Lucy Moore is Messy Church Team Leader for BRF and an Associate Missioner for Fresh Expressions. Lucy is author of *The Gospels Unplugged, The Lord's Prayer Unplugged, Topsy Turvy Christmas, Messy Church* and *Messy Church 2* and *Messy Crafts* (all Barnabas) and *All-Age Worship* (BRF 2010).

Messy Church is growing! Every month, families who have never set foot in a church before are enjoying Messy Church, and every month more Messy Churches are started all over the UK and worldwide. Messy Church is proving effective in sharing God's good news with families across denominations and church traditions. We estimate that some 100,000 people belong to Messy Churches—and the number is growing all the time. For more information about Messy Church, visit www.messychurch.org.uk.

Messy Church is enabled, resourced and supported by BRF (Bible Reading Fellowship), a Registered Charity, as one of its core ministries. BRF makes Messy Church freely available and derives no direct income from the work that we do to support it in the UK and abroad.

Would you be willing to support this ministry with your prayer and your giving? To find out more, please visit www.messychurch.org.uk/champions.

Barnabas
for
Children

Barnabas for Children® is a registered word mark and the logo is a registered device mark of The Bible Reading Fellowship.
Messy Church® is a registered word mark and the logo is a registered device mark of The Bible Reading Fellowship.

Text copyright © Lucy Moore 2006
Illustrations copyright © Mary Hall 2006
The author asserts the moral right
to be identified as the author of this work

Published by
The Bible Reading Fellowship
15 The Chambers, Vineyard
Abingdon, OX14 3FE
United Kingdom
Tel: +44 (0)1865 319700
Email: enquiries@brf.org.uk
Website: www.brf.org.uk
BRF is a Registered Charity

ISBN 978 1 84101 503 3
First published 2006
Reprinted 2007, 2008 (twice), 2009, 2010 (three times), 2011
10 9 8
All rights reserved

Acknowledgments
Unless otherwise stated, scripture quotations are taken from the Contemporary English Version of the Bible published by HarperCollins Publishers, copyright © 1991, 1992, 1995 American Bible Society.

Scripture quotations taken from The New Revised Standard Version of the Bible, Anglicized Edition, copyright © 1989, 1995 by the Division of Christian Education of the National Council of the Churches of Christ in the USA, are used by permission. All rights reserved.

Scripture quotations taken from the *Holy Bible, New International Version*, copyright © 1973, 1978, 1984, 1995 by International Bible Society. Used by permission of Hodder & Stoughton, a division of the Hachette Livre UK Group. All rights reserved. 'NIV' is a registered trademark of International Bible Society. UK trademark number 1448790.

A catalogue record for this book is available from the British Library

Printed in the UK by CPI Bookmarque, Croydon, CR0 4TD

Messy CHURCH

Fresh ideas for building a Christ-centred community

Lucy Moore

ACKNOWLEDGMENTS

Thanks to the whole Messy Church team, especially Lesley and Derek Baker, Denise, Alice and Jack Williams, Sarah and Rebecca Powers, Rose Chase, Jackie, Sophie, Greg, Harry and Maisie Tutt, Sonia and Jim Passingham, Richard Manterfield, Doreen Rann, Sharon and Bob Wheeler, Bob and Louise Woodward, Rebecca and Teresa Moncreaff, Catherine and Graham King, Vicki Turner, Melanie, Emma and Joe Wells, Vicky Worrall, Paul, Arthur and Judith Moore, Geoff and Linda Broome, Bill and Lori Barberini, Fred Mant, Steve and Luke Jackson, Clare and Ronnie Williams, Jeanette Wiseman, Annie Harding, Joe Harbour, Robert Shrimpton, Sharon Lane, Jan Smith and all the other members of St Wilf's and Westbrook who do so much to make Messy Church happen.

Thanks also to Captain Graham Nunn C.A. for invaluable help in bringing the music out of the Middle Ages, to Margaret Withers for enthusiasm and helpful criticism, to Fresh Expressions for supporting and encouraging us and, as ever, to the Barnabas team for... well... for everything they do.

For all those on the edge

Preface

It's 4.15 on a Thursday afternoon. The hall is buzzing with conversation. Around a table, adults and children burst into laughter as they wrestle with metallic tubing and googly eyes and their teenage helpers despair of ever creating the promised artefact. A toddler slaps green paint on to a huge sheet of card under the watchful eye of a granny (not sure if they're related or not—it doesn't really matter). A five-year-old watches wide-eyed as an enthusiastic leader shows her how to bang in a nail. There's a delicious smell wafting out of the kitchen. The ten-year-olds, intent on their glass-painting, agree it must be jacket potatoes. The vicar takes a photo of the surreal result of the junk modelling and two mums catch up on the gossip as they drink welcome cups of tea and slowly decorate gift bags while their children make something unidentifiable but very chocolatey upstairs. The cooks should be getting the plates stacked, but one of the mums needs to talk about her problems with her foster children. I would be panicking about the story for the celebration later, but there's a huge collage of the Great Banquet to assemble before five o' clock, the powder paint has proved a formidable weapon of mess creation in the hands of Jack, we've barely got started on the lettering and, whoops, someone's kicked over the glue pot… Just another Messy Church.

Contents

Thematic programmes for spring term

Thematic programmes for through the year

Foreword

All across Britain, something is happening. Christians are starting fresh expressions of church for those who are outside or on the edge of the Christian community. There are hundreds already. Some Christians start fresh expressions on purpose. Others begin almost by accident. Every single one is messy.

As a Church in Britain, there is a widespread sense that we are all learning new things as we look for what God is doing and try to join in. No one has all the answers (or even all the questions). No one is saying, 'There is one way to do this and it's my way.' There is a sense of helping one another and sharing the lessons one step at a time. The learning places are wherever God's people are stepping out in faith and doing a new thing.

Messy Church is one of those learning places. I'm delighted that Lucy and the team at Messy Church have been able to offer what they have learnt so far through this book. It's crammed with good things and there are delights on every page. As I read the text, I kept thinking of people I wanted to give it to: clergy and children's workers, church councils and young people. It's full of good fun, deep wisdom and practical know-how. *Messy Church* will be a blessing to many. I hope it leads to lots of mess and to many different forms of church.

Steven Croft
Bishop of Sheffield

Messy Church is featured on *expressions: the dvd*, which is a series of short stories introducing the idea of Fresh Expressions, showing the rich diversity of engagement and stories to be told. *expressions: the dvd 1* is published by Church House Publishing, priced £14.99.

Introduction

St Wilfrid's is an Anglican church in a suburban area of Portsmouth. It's an area that has to fight for any sense of community as the old village has been swallowed up in housing estates. There are many elderly people in the area and many young families. By and large it's a pretty comfortable area, neither massively well off nor deeply impoverished. The church has fantastic facilities, thanks to the vision and commitment to growth of the previous incumbent and congregations: two halls, kitchen, toilets and church all interlinked, with a car park and small garden. On a Sunday there are four services: a quiet 8 o'clock Communion, a traditional 9.30 Communion, an informal service at 11.15 with a small Junior Church, and an evening service. There used to be an annual holiday club for children, but when that stopped there was only the small Thursday night children's group that could be seen as any sort of opportunity for children in the parish to encounter God.

We sat down and thought hard about the direction we should head in, and what we came up with was Messy Church. This first part of the book looks at what it is and how it works, and suggests how you might go about thinking through the issues for your own situation.

Messy Church came out of the frustration of knowing that we had good premises, good leaders, some good ideas, but few children and families turning up on a Sunday. The realization that we simply weren't connecting was the starting point. I hope it will be a model as much in its many mistakes as in its successes. It's not meant to be a showcase perfect model to be copied slavishly (heaven forbid), but an example to learn from.

I also hope that the book will get your creative juices flowing and help you as you think about who the messy edges are in your church, and how you might reach them.

FRESH EXPRESSIONS

This is a book that starts to explore a particular 'fresh expression' of church. Fresh Expressions is a movement within the churches that seeks to show how churches are being church in different ways for different people and situations. You'll find inspiration and challenges in the growing directory of imaginative churches on their website: www.freshexpressions.org.uk.

It's been very frustrating to write this book, as new developments keep occurring in the Fresh Expressions movement—and even within Messy Church. Every month we come up with new ideas to try out and there's no way the book will be able to keep pace with them all. But it's a start, and arguably an appropriately messy one.

> **What defines a fresh expression of church? A fresh expression of church is intended as a community or congregation which is already (or has the potential to grow into) a church in its own right. It is not intended to be a halfway house or stepping stone for someone joining a Sunday morning congregation.**
> FRESH EXPRESSIONS WEBSITE

Is what we do a fresh expression of church, or is Messy Church just a club? It would be far easier to run a craft club! Far easier to swim with the cultural tide and avoid reminding people that they're more than material beings, that there's a personal God who loves them just as they are and wants them to get to know him better. Far easier not to make space for an encounter with God through worship as well as through creativity and friendship. Oh yes, far, far easier not to try to devise acts of worship that appeal to all ages, but merely to sink into a secular 'educational club' mode where our main aim is to develop fine motor skills and table manners. It would also be so much easier to get our hands on external funding if we didn't mention God!

Our vision, though, has always been to use the wonderful tools of creativity and food as a way of helping people come close to God and to each other. We don't want to hide behind a misleading name: we call it Messy Church up front, so that people have no illusions that it's just a social club. In our particular area, at this particular point in history, this is a fresh expression of church that is right for us.

Concept and considerations

CHAPTER 1

An overview of 'messy' theology

If nothing else, the *name* 'Messy Church' was an inspiration: it begs the question, 'What on earth is it?' and it makes people smile. The idea comes partly from the observation in Pete Ward's book, *Liquid Church* (Paternoster Press, 2002), that 'a liquid church will have fuzzy edges'.

Pete uses parents and toddler groups as an example of a network close to the church community when he says:

With the parents and tots we see that the network of connections spreads from those inside the church to those who may have no connection with regular Sunday worship. When we start to regard the network itself as church, then the notion of insiders and outsiders starts to break down. Instead, we have a network of communication and relationship where Christian love and mutual support form part of the flow. The boundaries have started to become more fuzzy and less well defined.
LIQUID CHURCH, PP. 47–48

There's a certain point at which a person might have friends in church, pray, attend the odd Communion service and try to make the annual jumble sale, but they'd think it strange to go to a house group or to be asked to put more than 50p in the collection bag. In the nicest possible sense, they're part of the messy edge, neither out nor in.

> **Church has moved from a central role in our society to the edges. At the same time, the 'centre' of our society is moving around. As churches, we need to learn to live at the edge again—to rebuild community there.**
>
> FRESH EXPRESSIONS WEBSITE

So networks are fuzzy and church is on the messy edge of the fuzzy networks. Life isn't tidy: one great strength of the Church of England is that it welcomes people on the messy edges without requiring them to decide whether they're in (so pay your tithe and sign up for ten weeks' heavy discipling) or out (so begone to outer darkness where there is wailing and gnashing of teeth)—and many other denominations work in the same way.

I suppose it's an apt reflection of the way many of us journey messily towards God. There might be 'road to Damascus' moments when we career in our spiritual Ferraris up the Autobahn to glory. Equally, there might be lots of gentle moments when God the Spirit nudges us a little further into his arms through a smile from a child, a moment of awe and wonder at the beauty of nature, a new thought about an old Bible story or a caring word from a fellow traveller. It's a messy way of working, but surely a Father God who can invent a sea cucumber and who is happy to work through people like me, like you, must have a creatively messy streak in him? His created world isn't renowned for its tidiness, after all: order and pattern, yes, but when did you last see a symmetrical tree that never shed a leaf? Jesus spent most of his time not at the tidy religious centre of Jerusalem, but out on the messy fringes of Jewish society among the ambiguous collaborators, the foreign settlers, the demi-monde of disreputable women and dodgy dealers, the scruffy disciples and mucky children.

Perhaps we would like people to be clear-cut: either a Christian or not, a member of the church or an outsider. Life would be so much easier. Yes, there comes a point when many of us can say for definite,

'Yup, I'm a Christian', with the same certainty that we can say, 'Yup, I'm married', but surely, on the way, the journey to faith involves bits of belonging, a little believing, a certain amount of ownership all swilling around together in a life-changing primeval soup while the Spirit works in us to bring us nearer to Jesus in our many different ways.

> **Post-Christendom churches will be messy communities where belonging, believing and behaving are in process rather than neatly integrated.**
> STUART MURRAY, *CHURCH AFTER CHRISTENDOM*, PATERNOSTER, P. 35

Oh yes.

Hmmm. If you juggle with this idea, you soon arrive at a church that not only *is* a joyful mess but which *makes* a mess joyfully. While the second half of this book contains outlines for sessions on art and craft for people who want the basis of a ready-made programme, the book's main intention is to kickstart some thinking about what particular form your fresh expression of church might take. Your end product will have a creative impulse and drive if it comes from your own prayer, people, needs, talents and assets rather than if you simply lift what we've come up with here.

Why not Sunday?

Why does the church need to put on something extra midweek for people on the edge? Why not simply expect them to come along to church on a Sunday? After all, many Sunday services are modern, friendly, use up-to-date language and have activities for the children.

Well, there are several problems with Sunday church. Here are a few.

It's on Sunday. For many people who don't come to church, Sunday is now a day for family, sport and shopping. It may be the only day that families have together. It may be the day we visit Grandma. It may be when separated parents send the children off to the other parent at the other end of the country for the weekend. Rugby trials, football practice, netball tournaments, swimming competitions—children will be involved in all sorts of leisure activities on a Sunday, and church will have to be on a par with Disneyland to compete if the adults in the family aren't already committed Christians.

It 'belongs to someone else'. I had a taste of what it must be like, coming into a church for the first time, when we went to cheer on a friend who was performing at a folk club in West Yorkshire. Suddenly we hadn't the foggiest idea how to behave. Could we just walk in or should we knock? What was expected of us? Could we sit anywhere or were some seats reserved for regulars? Could we talk during the singing? Could we go and get a drink from the bar while music was playing? Were we expected to sing along, or muse silently on the performance, like in a theatre? Would anyone speak to us? It was very disorientating, even irritating, to feel so wrong-footed, like a foreign tourist. However friendly our churches are, there can be a feeling for the outsider that this is an alien culture with so many unwritten expectations that it's too risky to set foot over the threshold. Church is not even part of the wallpaper of most people's lives any more, and fewer and fewer people are automatically at home in a church. *But what if church were a place where the 'outsiders' helped to set the expectations?*

A Sunday service may have a great deal invested in it already. Is Sunday church designed for the insider or the outsider? It's very hard to put on a service that meets the needs of both regular committed Christians and those on the messy edge. There are so many needs. For a lifelong churchgoer there may be a need to sing a favourite hymn, which happens to be full of such complex theology that a newcomer is totally bewildered.

Oh generous love! that he, who smote
In Man for man the foe,
The double agony in man
For man should undergo.

CARDINAL J.H. NEWMAN, *HYMNS ANCIENT AND MODERN REVISED*

Brilliant hymn; sung it all my life; I find more in it every time I sing it. But it's not Radio Two, is it?

Ironically, church liturgical rules can also make barriers between a visitor and God. Take saying the Collect every week in an Anglican church, for example—a massively long single sentence, describing God for three lines with four-syllable words, squeezing in the nugget of a request in the middle and finishing off (with barely a pause for a comma) with another three lines of doxology. Is this designed for a *Sun* reader? Or a six-year-old? Or me? Which of us can remember what we've prayed for by the end of it? How long does the Eucharistic Prayer seem to an eight-year-old... or to someone with chronic back pain?

From the other point of view, is a child-friendly sermon what a committed adult disciple needs every week? Does every song have to be simple to the point of simplistic? *Are they going to make me clap?* (Before you panic, Graham Nunn has selected the songs for the celebration services in this book and 'dumbing down' does not enter into his accessible and thoughtful selection.) Yes, there are gifted worship leaders and speakers who can appeal to all ages simultaneously. But not everyone can, and it would be unfair to expect them to, for all sorts of reasons: personal aptitude, habits, gaps in theological training, among others. Leading an all-age service is more difficult than you think until you've tried it.

While I love the principle of a service where all people from all backgrounds and ages worship tolerantly together, there is a massive gap between the needs of someone putting a toe in the church pond and someone who's already ploughing up and down in it like an Olympic swimmer. Sunday's may not be the easiest service to adapt as there is so much invested in it for so many people. We need to know when we should be down on our knees fighting for change and when we would just be stubbing our toes against an immovable object. The ongoing challenge for us with Messy Church is to create a true church, not to see it as a halfway house to Sundays.

The place of children in your church may be unclear. Many churches welcome children and provide for them to worship God appropriately. Some still feel uncomfortable about where they fit in. 'We love to have the children here...' can include an unspoken get-out clause: '... as long as they're quiet and well-behaved and do what we do.' If children are happy in church, parents are happier to come. If children are happy in church, they are more likely to keep coming through the difficult tweenage years and to keep bringing along their friends. Does your church have a rule of thumb of welcoming and respecting children or are children seen as a necessary evil? If you changed Sunday services to make them more child-friendly, how would the rest of the congregation react? Is it a cop-out or common sense to design a fresh new approach to whole-family worship at another time of the week? (This is a genuine question, not a rhetorical one: we are for ever wrestling with the ideal versus the workable!)

But isn't Sunday sacrosanct?

Many Christians feel that Sunday is the right time to come together to worship. It is the new sabbath, the day of rest. It's an opportunity for the whole church family to come together. Ho hum. I'm put in mind of the line from 'King of glory' that used to puzzle me terribly as a child:

> Seven whole days, not one in seven,
> I will praise thee.
> GEORGE HERBERT, *HYMNS ANCIENT AND MODERN REVISED*

(Of course I couldn't work out why the writer was so peevishly determined not to praise God even for one day in seven.)

God is a God who bursts out of compartments. Christians can't keep holiness just for Sundays. It must shine out into the whole of life, so that every part is holy for this 'royal priesthood', this 'holy nation' of believers—holiness in the ordinary, if you like. There is no reason why worship offered on a Thursday should be any less worship than that offered on a Sunday. Where the difficulty comes is in the established congregation's perception of the Thursday congregation and the Thursday congregation's perception of themselves. Is it a church in its own right? We'll look at this later on.

To consider

✤ Is Sunday the best time of the week for the people you are trying to reach?
✤ Try going to an established club or group to feel what it's like to be an outsider. What would make you go back?
✤ Is there so much invested in a Sunday service as it stands that to change it would be too painful for the 'regulars'?
✤ Look at your service through the eyes of a child. Which parts of it help them come closer to God?

O God, grant us the serenity to accept what cannot be changed, the courage to change what can be changed and the wisdom to know the difference.
REINHOLD NIEBUHR

CHAPTER 2

What is Messy Church?

Messy Church is a once-monthly time when families come together to enjoy being together, making things together, eating together and celebrating God together through his word, through music and through prayer. It's different from a children's activity day because it's an event for children and their carers or parents together, and it's more than a local authority fun day because of the element of worship that underpins it all.

With Messy Church we are trying to be a worshipping community of all ages, centred on Christ, showing Christian hospitality—giving people a chance to express their creativity, to sit down together to eat a meal and have fun within a church context.

Our principles, in no particular order, are:

✣ To provide an opportunity for people of all ages to worship together.
✣ To help people of all ages to feel that they belong in church and to each other.
✣ To help people have fun together.
✣ To give people a chance to express their God-given creativity.
✣ To invite people into an experience of Christian community.
✣ To introduce people to Jesus through hospitality, friendship, stories and worship.

The session runs something like this:

3.30	Doors open. People arrive, play board games and have a drink and biscuit
4.00–5.00	Craft time
5.00–5.15	Celebration service in church
5.15–5.45	Hot meal together

THE COMPONENT PARTS OF MESSY CHURCH

Welcome

The session starts at 3.30, but we don't begin the craft time until 4.00. The thinking is that, if people want to, they can come straight from picking their children up from school and save a journey home and back again, but there is also time to go home and get changed if they want to. During the first half hour, we serve tea, coffee, squash and biscuits and have a variety of games set out on the tables and floor: board games, jigsaws, colouring, word searches, table football and so on.

Everyone signs in as they arrive (so that we have a list in case of fire) and writes their name on a sticker. We encourage helpers to have their crafts set up and ready before 3.30 so that they can join in with the games and get to know people better. The temptation in Messy Church is to be busy doing jobs and to forget that the real work is in making friends with everyone who comes, young and old. We also put a 'donations' bowl by the sign-in list. It's nice to be able to offer everything for free as a gesture of hospitality, but it's also nice for people to feel that they are giving as well as taking. So we leave it up to the individuals concerned. You might do it differently.

At about 4.00, one of the team climbs on to a chair and welcomes everyone very briefly, says what the day's theme is and gives a quick rundown of the crafts on offer. We keep this very short, as people are there to have fun, not listen to us droning on.

Craft

Between 4.00 and 5.00, everyone goes free range to do as much or as little craft and art as they want. We have about ten tables set up round our two halls, with an adult, teenage or child leader at each to show all comers what to do. Child and teen helpers are great, but it's best to have several of them responsible, so that they all get a chance to go off and have fun at the other tables as well as running their own. Our third-agers are brilliant at leading crafts too: you should see the surreal ideas Bob and Louise come up with, or the way Doreen (a great-grandmother) gets alongside the most timid of children.

In each unit of this book (the 'thematic programmes') there are ten craft ideas. They are almost all very basic, easy things to make, each taking around 5–10 minutes. We have found that people want to do lots of short activities rather than a few long ones. This is frustrating because you can't actually learn many new skills in a five-minute slot, but they are all fun to do. We are not afraid to repeat some craft activities. Put together in a book like this, two lots of stone-painting seems needlessly unimaginative, but if you're only holding the sessions once a month, it's a very long time since people last did it.

We try to have a range of things to make that include all the senses. The food option is always very popular, but we put someone dragon-like in charge of this, who will not only make sure hands are washed *'with soap!'* beforehand, but will also be strict about apportioning quantities of ingredients. Otherwise the first three children eat all the jelly teddies.

Something we've noticed is that the parents of the older children sometimes feel awkward about joining in the crafts as their children are so independent that they don't need or want Mum making stuff with them all the time. So we try to lay on something that these parents can do as they sit and chat to each other—something that's a little more delicate and satisfying for them than getting their new top covered in poster paint. That way, they can still have fun making things, and their children can join in with them if they want, rather than the other way around. For example, we had some pretty gift bags for them to decorate with cut-outs, and we bought some glass-painting pens so that they could decorate bottles and pop some bath salts in them, all to sell at the church fair. It's satisfying, allows the creative impulse full rein and is useful as well.

Worship

It is worth putting dedicated energy into the worship as this may be the only time in the month that many of the people who come to Messy Church have a chance to worship. Our celebration is held in church and is a very short service to celebrate some aspect of God, based on a theme that has been picked up in the crafts. Details of some ideas are included in the session outlines. The Barnabas website also has lots of additional ideas for worship that includes children (see www.barnabasinchurches.org.uk).

As with all the Messy Church ideas in this book, some of them we already do, some we know we should but haven't yet got organized to do, and some we know we'll never manage in a month of Thursdays, but they are Jolly Good Ideas all the same and if we had a dedicated family worker we would certainly do them. Had we but space enough and time... So I offer them tentatively, hoping that if you visit us, you won't expect to see everything in place. Like a building site, it's still all a bit... well... messy.

We try to keep in mind that most of what people experience in a church situation comes not from a sermon but from non-verbal messages. It comes from what we see, hear, smell and touch, from the way we are greeted (or not) and from the expectations and behaviour of the people around us.

Coming into the worship space

Traditionally, churches have a greeter or welcomer on the door to be the human face of the love of God. With a service full of 'extended family members' who may not come into church otherwise, if you are holding the act of worship in your church building it is doubly important to have someone to greet everyone as they come in. We used to just pile into church after the craft, but now we gather in the hall and move in a ramshackle but definitely processional throng. As we get more organized, we'll try out banners… ribbons… instruments… a good marching song?

It might also be helpful to have some 'sidespeople' to help people find an appropriate place to sit. Away from the rigours of Sunday services or school assemblies, the expectations are different and children especially need gentle but firm help to know what is appropriate in church. Do we want them perched in the pulpit? If not, we'll have to make it clear, as the pulpit is a delightful place to choose to sit when you're six. Do we expect adults to sit with their children and supervise them? A lot of the older children will want to sit with their friends instead and we can't rely on parental super-vision. The expectations come from our team and, if they're all laying tables or clearing up their craft, they won't be able to set many of those standards of behaviour.

Whether or not you are using your church building for the act of worship, look at your worship space with a child's eyes. Is the furniture a comfortable size for short-legged people? Where will the pushchairs go? What hazards are there? How would I feel about coming into it if I were a child? Is it warm enough for a young baby or an elderly person? Is it clean enough for toddlers to crawl in?

We'd like to think about changing the worship setting slightly every time so that there is continuity with variety. Perhaps there could be something new to look at as everyone enters: a picture at the front, a thematic decoration along the seats, a focal table with something thematic on it to inspire awe and wonder.

Music is also important in creating an atmosphere: a CD playing or live instrumentalists have very different effects. We have to decide whether it's better to have people singing as they come in or whether they would be more at home having a chance to chat and find their seat without worrying about song words. Perhaps the music is stilling and peaceful, or uplifting.

The smell of a church or worship space can also be something to think about. Sometimes it might be appropriate to have oil burners, incense, or aromatic foods, which can all help to create different atmospheres.

Children also like to have something to do with themselves in the messy time while everyone's finding a seat.

✢ Singing a song.
✢ Watching a candle.
✢ Finding a story in the pew Bible for later.
✢ Watching a PowerPoint show of photos of the crafts they've just made, or a short clip of video (*Veggietales*, for example, or one of the ones that show action praise songs, such as Doug Horley's).

A puppet making an appearance over the edge of a pulpit or lectern will keep incoming children gleeful for those difficult minutes.

The service itself

We keep it simple. We keep it as participative as possible. We tie everything to the theme to bring it home in a variety of ways. We keep it real.

Keep it simple. While teenagers love high-tech effects, black boxes with knobs on, screens and flashing lights, children don't need all that. Children also enjoy interaction, human contact, live people or puppets, quietness as well as (and sometimes more than) noise. They love story, drama and singing—activities that involve them and feed their imagination.

A simple story, well told, will stick with adults and children more than all the flashy effects we could afford. Find your church story-tellers and wheel them in.

Keep it participative. Wherever possible, we avoid the one-man show, expecting everyone else to sit meekly in their pew. We get everyone involved as much as possible. Children get to know God through movement as well as stillness, through play as well as prayer, through their hands and feet as well as through their intellect. (And adults...?)

So, for all aspects of the service—in the teaching, the prayer, the singing—we try to provide opportunities for everyone to be looking at things, holding things, touching things, imagining, joining in. We weave in opportunities for people to discuss a question in groups, to produce a drawing, prayer or other offering together. This reinforces the way that we are here together, not just as individuals but as a big family.

Tie everything to the theme: We need to provide plenty of reinforcement to help people remember what the theme is all about. We make everything visual, using OHPs or digital projectors, books, pictures or objects. We make ourselves tie all aspects of the service in with the theme.

We give free rein to our creativity. How, for example, can we do prayers related to the parable of the farmer (Mark 4:1–8)? Could we all imagine tiny seeds in our hand, imagine that they are the things we have to offer God and mime planting them as an offering of all that we have to him? Could we write or draw prayers on seed-shaped cards and place them in a cardboard field at the front? Could we plant actual seeds for each prayer offered and let them grow for next time? Could we devise a short series of hand movements showing sowing, nurturing and harvesting, giving thanks for the good things that God has given us, saying sorry for the way we don't use them properly and asking for our lives to give good harvests?

There's a fantastic list of imaginative ways of praying on page 75 of *Creating a Learning Church* by Margaret Cooling (BRF, 2005).

Keep it real. We keep the transcendent truths about God related to the concrete realities of people's lives: we keep it real. We lose all the churchy jargon except when it helps people and when we can be sure they understand it. Even the innocuous 'Please be seated' has a pretty pompous ecclesiastical ring when you think about it: why not just say, 'Please sit down'? We keep relating the story or passage to the lives of the people there with us. What has this story got to say to them? Why should they care about this hairy historical bloke crossing the Reed Sea? What on earth has a vine or a shepherd got to do with their life in suburban Portsmouth? We use real examples from local life and modern-day situations, resetting the stories if necessary: 'A man was going down London Road late one night when some drunks from the Spotted Cow beat him up…' Jesus used places and characters that his listeners would instantly understand, and we need to do the same.

Having said this, rites and ritual are important, especially for young children, so we try to keep some parts of the service that are always the same—the welcome or the blessing, for example. We frame quiet moments as well as noisy ones. We try to help people to have a moment when they can feel they are in the palm of God's hand.

Think about which parts of your usual service might help these people draw close to God. What about the Lord's Prayer? The Creed? Confession and absolution? The Eucharist? The Psalms? An Old and New Testament reading? Are these crucial building blocks that you feel you must have every time or valuable ingredients to be used once in a while? Or are they always inappropriate for use within this context? We don't try to include a full *Common Worship* liturgy in 15 minutes. We're selective and do less but try to do it well.

A basic shape that works well for us is:

✣ Opening song
✣ Story or illustration
✣ Response song
✣ Prayer
✣ Grace

Although the celebration is usually led by the vicar, this is only because the rest of us are up to our ears in craft and cooking and he's free to concentrate on that one part of the whole session. (He's also quite good at it.) Often, though, parts (or all) of the celebration are led by different laypeople.

Messy Church invites us to be creative in our worship. Of course, we'll make mistakes, just as an artist or composer makes mistakes during the creative process, but it's far better to try and get it wrong than never to try at all. Surely that would be true failure.

Perhaps the 2005 Persil adverts are near the mark, when they show people of all ages in different activities that entail their clothes getting filthy, and claim that what matters isn't the dirt but the intensity of emotion or creative pioneering that is behind the dirt. By extension, staying tidily in our pews, in well-behaved ranks, is not in itself a virtue. Having the guts to find ways to worship God in spirit and in truth might involve a certain amount of creative chaos. It will certainly involve failure at times.

> **Over time, it's obviously our goal to decrease our failure rate and to take calculated risks because of all we have learned. But we'll never be able to say goodbye to failure altogether if we choose to aim for creativity. It's part of the deal.**
>
> NANCY BEACH, WRITING ABOUT WILLOW CREEK CHURCH, IN *AN HOUR ON SUNDAYS*, ZONDERVAN, 2004, P. 182

There is also the interesting question of how the midweek Messy Church people relate to those who worship on a Sunday. The two need to know how much they belong to each other and how much they need each other. For us, this issue is still work-in-progress. We should pray for Sunday people on Thursdays and vice versa. We should occasionally have display boards showing each group what the others are up to. We should make sure that those who only attend Messy Church have the same access to the prayer structures (the prayer requests e-mailing list, for example) that the rest of the church family has. Do they know how to buy a parish magazine? If they needed to, would they know who to talk to about problems or spiritual matters?

Do we flag up carefully selected church events to the Messy Church people: the socials, the Alpha suppers, the parenting courses, the Emmaus course, the Confirmation course? Can we persuade someone from the pastoral team to be on hand simply to chat and get to know Messy Church people month by month, so that if crises arise, the relationship is already there? There are so many opportunities. We're not managing to make the most of them yet, but bit by bit we will get round to turning them into more than just good ideas.

It's interesting to imagine how messy ancient Old Testament Jewish worship must have been: the animals and birds on the altar, crumbled cakes with oil poured over the top, fires, water sloshing around, incense smoking away, fat and kidneys being butchered up, the priest showering everyone with blood from the sacrifice. You only have to read the opening chapters of Leviticus to see that God's priority cannot be a clean carpet. We'd never get away with that level of mess in our church: the wardens would have kittens. Surely God doesn't notice mess in that sense. What God notices is how the worship is honouring to him and how it draws people closer to him. Our responsibility isn't to make worship neat and tidy but to make it the best we can offer and as genuine, relevant, living and Christ-centred as we are able to—and to have the graciousness to exercise our ministry of hoovering afterwards.

We started by holding the celebration after the food, but swapped them round eventually, as some people were leaving as soon as they'd eaten their cake and we wanted to give everyone every excuse to make space for worship in their busy lives. The advantage of finishing with food is that everyone stays until the end and gets to participate in the key point: the worship. The advantage of finishing with the worship is that it makes a clear 'dismissal': a point when everyone knows it's time to leave. Also, the kitchen helpers can get cleared up more quickly.

Churches can enhance the sense of identity within their different congregations by considering some of the following dynamics. The more these are in place, the stronger and healthier will be the sense that each congregation is a 'church' in itself:

✣ Establish a planned and consistent divergence of worship style—for example, an afternoon Taizé congregation, or a service for parents and toddlers, or strongly choir-led worship.
✣ Grow a dedicated and recognized leadership for each.
✣ Establish a particular mission focus for the differing congregations. This might be an age-related focus, or geographical responsibility within a large parish, or by concern for a local social issue.
✣ Provide discrete pastoral care structures for each congregation, which are known by them.
✣ Deny and refuse all language that calls one of the congregations 'the main congregation'.
✣ Create an overall team or group ministry in which each congregation has fair representation.

One danger of a multiple congregation approach is that it is often heavily influenced by the worship needs of those who already come. Care must be taken to adopt a clear missionary approach, and seek to connect with a community outside the church, instead of simply using a multiple congregation approach as a way of trying to keep the existing church members happy.

JOHN HULL, *MISSION-SHAPED CHURCH*, CHP, 2004, PP. 59–62

Food

We didn't want anyone to have to turn out for Messy Church straight after school, be busy with the children for two hours and then go home and need to cook tea, so we try to provide the sort of meal that a family might have at home on a school night—even including vegetables. Check out the recipe section of this book for some basic ideas that don't cost a bomb. Each meal has a serving suggestion with it in the individual units, as we've found through trial and error (mostly error) that getting hot food out to large numbers is more complicated than it sounds.

Cake is our traditional pudding and saves washing up another bowl or plate. We ask each helper to bring a cake with them. For our first birthday party, one of the twelve-year-old members, Sophie, asked if she could make and decorate the birthday cake—it was far better than anything we would have made. However, having said all that, there are times when we're short of leaders and it's a choice between easy food or cancelling Messy Church. A summer Messy Church was a great success when the food consisted of boil-up hot-dogs, crisps, cheapo choc-ices and fruit. It was all eaten outside as a big picnic and there were only the hot-dog pans to wash up. Splendid!

It might sound intimidating, even impossible, to sort out a hot meal for a large group. We're blessed with a big kitchen and a dishwasher (oh bliss), even if the gas cooker is temperamental to the point of lunacy, but in some church halls I've worked in, there's been one dodgy microwave and a wobbly sink. Yes, we panic on a regular basis as we dish out platefuls to anything between 60 and 90 people, ranging from ravenous teenagers to picky toddlers, but if you decide that eating together is worth doing for the way it brings people together, you will find a manageable way of doing it. You might not feel able to cook shepherd's pie for 60 but could six of you each cook enough for ten people? Could everyone bring a plateful of sandwiches to share? Could every family pitch in some money for fish and chips, or could you dial up a pizza or two? Could you simply have a cake break and sit down together to enjoy them?

There is something sacred about eating together, however little is actually on the plates. I also wonder if some of the children ever sit down at a table together as a family. Perhaps, for some, Messy Church is the only occasion when they do.

We always begin with Messy Church Grace. Our version needs three fingers in the air. Turn your hand round 180 degrees with each number and put fingers up or down to go with the numbers, saying, '3, 2, 1; 1, 2, 3; Thank you, God, for all our tea.' You can find different graces by doing a search on the net for 'children's graces'.

To address the problem I mentioned earlier of 'How do people know when to leave at the end of the meal?' we've introduced the birthday slot at the cake stage of the meal. It's a time to call out anyone, young or old, who's had a birthday in the last month, to sing a special blessing version of 'Happy Birthday' to them and give them a small present. This not only gives individuals a special place in the gathering, but signals a gentle 'Thank you very much, hope you've enjoyed it, see you next month and you might like to think about going home now' moment.

Variety

While it's good to have a standard session outline, we're learning the need to keep ringing the changes as well. Every now and then, we try to introduce something a little different from normal. This might be because of necessity: on the summer day when we had very few leaders available, we got everyone to do just four activities and to do them all together. This had the effect of getting people more involved and talking to each other. Alternatively, it may be seasonal: we had a special ceremony during the meal for Easter, to echo the Passover meal. It was a simple question-and-answer ritual about the different foods on the table.

Other seasonal festivals are opportunities to ring the changes and mark them out as something special with a break in routine. Harvest might include a harvest procession to a field or carrying gifts to a retirement home. The meal might include a specially baked roll for each person and a short meditation on bread as it is eaten. Christmas, of course, provides plenty of opportunity for celebrations loud and quiet. One Christmas, Messy Church included a disco run by the youth group as their 'bit' for the community. It might be fun to hold the whole thing out-of-doors one week, perhaps if you're looking at one of the 'outside' stories, such as the feeding of the five thousand or the Sermon on the Mount. Another surprise might be to organize games for the first half hour, with a parachute or a bouncy castle, or invite a dance or drama leader in to share their skills.

CHAPTER 3

The aims of
Messy Church

AIMING TO BE A WORSHIPPING COMMUNITY

We deliberately included worship within the Messy Church structure, even though it's often difficult to plan and lead. We wanted to give everyone an experience of the spiritual side of life, a space to meet God through worship together. It also means that we're not tempted to see Messy Church as a mere feeder into Sunday church. It's a valid worshipping congregation in its own right and we are delighted and honoured that people of all ages come and enjoy themselves in a church context.

On the principle that we're all on a faith journey, we keep an eye open for what the next step might be for us all, both Sunday worshippers and Thursday (Messy Church) worshippers. Perhaps, for some, an invitation to a Christian parenting course might be appropriate. For some, perhaps the best route might be an invitation to join a house group, to get involved with other aspects of church life, like the youth group or the adult social groups, or maybe to come along to an Alpha group or evangelistic event with other Christians. Messy Church is designed to give people the opportunity to worship, make friends and explore their creativity within a Christian frame-work. We try to make it a place where people can grow in faith through a mixture of belonging and believing. The questioning and owning will probably happen elsewhere.

'Let every living creature praise the Lord' (Psalm 150:6).

AIMING TO BE ALL-AGE

We are firmly convinced that our society and our churches need to be all-age. In our society in the UK we need things to do that the whole family can enjoy together, learning from each other, from babies to great-grandparents. Theme parks describe themselves as a 'great family day out'—yes, if Dad likes sliding down a helter-skelter or Mum's idea of a thrill is going round the *Wind in the Willows* animated scenes five times. Church should make a massive effort to buck the trend. This is how we're meant to live: in community— what Kathryn Copsey calls 'the healthy village of the church' (*From the Ground Up*, Barnabas, 2005). Living a long way from my own parents, I know the benefit that my children receive from the warm hugs of the substitute grannies in our church and the wealth of experience we all gain from rubbing shoulders week by week with babies, teenagers, Navy officers, hurting adults, families from Africa, happy people, those who are unwell, toddlers, guide dog trainers, drummers, carers, painters, speech therapists... The list of 'healthy village members' is unending and gives us far more than we can provide from the small resources of our nuclear family.

We fail all the time. We wanted to provide art activities that adults would learn from as much as the children, but are still working on that one: the adults want to concentrate far longer than the children are able to and the activities veer towards things that children can achieve, rather than the delicate quilling and calligraphy that adults could take home with pride. We aim our food more towards children's palates than adults'. How lovely it would be to have a glass of wine with a leisurely three-course meal. No chance! Yet people will come and enjoy being together if they feel that they are among friends. So we keep trying to work towards building relationships, reminding the team that what matters isn't a perfectly glued collage but getting to know names and really listening to the people who come and join in the activity. If the plates don't get cleared up quite as quickly because you're sitting chatting to a single mum or a garrulous five-year-old, does it really matter? It's good to remind the team of Martha and Mary!

> 'God had made the people very happy, and so on that day they celebrated and offered many sacrifices. The women and children joined in the festivities, and joyful shouts could be heard far from the city of Jerusalem' (Nehemiah 12:43).

AIMING TO BE CHRIST-CENTRED

One issue we wrestle with, with regard to Messy Church, is the question 'Is this just a club or is it a church?' We've come to believe that the difference between a club and a church is that a club is a group of people joined by a common interest, but a church, in the words of Archbishop Rowan Williams, 'is what happens when people encounter the risen Jesus and commit themselves to sustaining and deepening that encounter in their encounter with each other' (from the Foreword to *Mission-Shaped Church*.)

If what we are doing in Messy Church is Christ-centred, using our common interest in craft as a springboard into a deeper understanding of God, of each other and of his world, we are on the way to being church. If we can use our common interest as a bridge between people on the messy edges of the church and a relationship with Jesus and with his family of believers, we are on the way to being church.

According to the best available research, approximately 60% of the British population are probably beyond the reach of the churches. This proportion is much higher in urban areas and among the under forties. It is increasing year by year. Many people in this group have a belief in God; many are interested in spiritual things and in Christian spirituality. But the gap between where they are now and church is too wide to be easily crossed.

FRESH EXPRESSIONS WEBSITE

The lovely thing is that we all meet on the bridge on equal ground. The common ground is a shared interest in craft (or a shared longing for something to do with the children that doesn't involve a screen or joystick). It's not 'our' territory as traditional church can seem to an outsider, with the incomprehensible songs, the inexplicable standing, kneeling and sitting, the unwritten rules about being silent or joining in. No, we meet on equal terms as fellow splodgers, stickers and scribblers, the home team as messy as the newcomers, and in everything we do, we try to be Christ and show Christ.

The question is whether all those who come are committed to sustaining and developing that encounter with Christ, and I'm sure that many of them are not. But then, I might say the same of Sunday worshippers. We will look at this question in more depth in the next chapter, 'What is church?'

'Try to shine as lights among the people of this world, as you hold firmly to the message that gives life' (Philippians 2:15–16).

AIMING TO BE HOSPITABLE

Food plays a big part in Messy Church, as something sacred happens when human beings sit down and eat with each other. 'Sacred' may seem a strange word to use of a meal where 50 under-13s (and some over-40s) are vying for the bun with the most icing, but it's true. Perhaps it's because it's one of the signs of the kingdom—the banquet, the feast, the breaking of bread. Eating together gives more opportunity for building friendships, and providing a meal for friends and strangers expresses something of God's open-handed generosity. Even if you only feel able to provide a cup of tea and a biscuit, do think hard about how you can eat together as God's people. Perhaps, what the mission-shaped church needs is more paid church caterers than youth workers!

'When you eat or drink or do anything else, always do it to honour God' (1 Corinthians 10:31).

AIMING TO BE CREATIVE

Messing about with paint and glue is an action that taps into the very question of what it is to be human. We are made in the image of God, and God is the great Creator. As we create and play together, we echo his playful creativity and we are renewed and repaired ourselves. So what, if God designs with supernovae and we design with last week's yoghurt pots? Something in our spirituality is restored as our creativity chimes with his. Our team struggle to stay creative in their approach, to think up fresh ideas and structures, to treat crises as creative opportunities and to see every encounter as a chance to build the kingdom, pebble by pebble, conversation by conversation, and bun by bun.

'So God created humans to be like himself' (Genesis 1:27).

What is church?
A theological reflection

Perhaps because food is such an integral part of Messy Church, the story of the feeding of the five thousand (Luke 9:10–17) makes a good starting point for reflection on what we're trying to do—and I think it's quite revealing. What sort of gathering are we in Messy Church? A full-blown church of rock-solid disciples or something different? Something... messier?

Perhaps the feeding of the five thousand isn't just a story about miracles. Perhaps it's about the question 'What is a disciple?' You've got 5000 men, plus women and children (who don't even deserve counting, but we will pass swiftly over this without grumbling), who have come together to hear Jesus. Are they disciples?

The poor old faithful, signed-on-the-dotted-line, yes-we-definitely-are disciples want to be alone with Jesus for a cosy post-mission huddle. Jesus, who has not only just heard the news about his cousin John's death but has also been having a bit of a ding-dong with the Pharisees, sneaks off with his twelve close friends for some time out in the countryside. It's all set to be a good time of small group fellowship—a retreat, a time to be close to God. Perhaps, in our Sunday churches, we would secretly rather be like that—a little cosy select group, keeping Jesus to ourselves. What do we feel at heart when someone from outside joins us? Is there that feeling of 'Oh bother, it's not half as cosy when a stranger comes in. They'll change everything'?

Yes, the crowds find out where Jesus is hiding and present

themselves for another Jesus Show. Perhaps they were there already, waiting by the lakeside. I can imagine the disciples' hearts sinking as they saw the crowds start to wave and shout from the shore. Or perhaps, as John says, the crowd arrived afterwards. It's hard not to picture them descending on the little group with whoops of glee at finding them at last, like the seekers in a game of hide-and-seek.

With bucketfuls of compassion at their sheep-like behaviour, Jesus 'welcomed them. He spoke to them about God's kingdom and healed everyone who was sick' (Luke 9:11). Then, of course, he gave them tea. Look at all that giving! There's not a hint that Jesus demanded anything of them. He just gave them his welcome, his wisdom, his powers and a slap-up picnic. Here's the free food prophecy of Isaiah 55:1–2 coming true: 'If you don't have any money, come, eat what you want! ... Listen carefully to me, and you will enjoy the very best foods.' Here is the manna from heaven being poured out free of charge. Jesus does make demands of his disciples—'You give them something to eat!' (Luke 9:13)—but not of the crowd. If only we, in our tired, busy world, would echo his unconditional pouring out of all that we are and all that we have. No wonder the outsiders stayed around.

Looking at the crowd on that hillside, we see a gathering of people of all ages, eager to see something of Jesus, but on an 'I'll take it or leave it' basis. Perhaps they were like the people described in *Mission-shaped Church* as 'open de-churched' (p. 37): people who 'have left church at some point but are open to return if suitably contacted and invited'. The people on the hillside were open. They were hungry to be fed spiritually. Even if they turned up hoping for a spectacular bit of water-into-wine or cleansing of lepers, they didn't leave the minute the miracles stopped and the teaching started. They had a God-shaped hole in them, even if they had been starved spiritually all their lives.

Were they disciples, though? Most of them must have been there to 'suck it and see'. They were making no commitment to Jesus beyond making the journey to see him and suffering a bruised bottom from sitting on a rock all day. I wonder if their obvious lack of food supplies was an indication that they weren't expecting to stay the whole day but somehow got caught up in his wonderful teaching? ('Can't we just stay for one more story, Mum?') The crowd on the hillside was a gathering of people. They certainly met Jesus there. There were people who were healed (Matthew 14:14) and who lapped up his teaching (Mark 6:34), and they broke bread together. But let's face it, there's not much evidence that the people in that crowd were committed to Jesus or to each other. We don't know if they were prepared to follow his teaching or if they were linked into any wider framework of faith.

The crowd is rather like the field that has wheat and weeds growing in it (Matthew 13:24–29), a mixture of the genuine and the bogus, those who will prove fruitful and those for whom it was just a good day out. Jesus is content for the field to be a messy mixture for the time being. He doesn't demand anything right there. He just gives what he has to give, and shows the people, in the messiest possible way (oily fish, crumbly bread passed from unwashed hand to hand; health and safety, eat your heart out!) how their lives can be transformed if they're in the hands of this miraculous God. It's a gospel of getting your hands mucky, of full bellies and uncontrollable laughter.

Obviously, this is only one side of the gospel, and discipline and suffering are the flipside of the fun and fellowship, but perhaps some churches need an excuse to rediscover the *fun* of following Jesus, that great party-thrower of banquets, picnics and intimate family suppers. Maybe, where we are with Messy Church is there on the hillside, outside the traditional church restrictions, with all the fun and froth of faith, the generous giving and the family fellowship. We're providing a picnic where people are free to come, take and go if that's what they want. Like God's provision of manna in a desolate land, Messy Church provides a source of nourishment, creativity and fellowship in a numb, materialistic society.

In our communities today, there are plenty of people who are searching spiritually and physically. There are people of all ages with spiritual needs, who feel 'there must be more to life than this' or who have a sense of something greater than an XBOX 360 or a widescreen

TV. There are plenty of people who have definite physical needs, too: they need a good solid meal, or perhaps a hug, a conversation where they're really listened to or the chance to put their feet up and have a cup of tea in peace. Maybe, when they meet both Jesus and his people together with that cup of tea, they'll stay longer than they'd planned. Not disciples, then. Not ready to take up their cross, any more than the sacrifice of time and effort to get to Messy Church and having to wash a pile of paint-splattered school jumpers, but they are followers on the messy edge, willing to hear more about Jesus.

The story of the feeding of the five thousand also has something to tell us about receiving from unlikely people. In John's version, it is the boy who gives up his picnic, and Jesus is able to feed everyone from this small gift. This passage says something to us about the way we treat children and other people who are traditionally sidelined. We, the organizers, the 'efficient', the 'skilled' ones, must expect to receive from them. We must keep our eyes and minds and hearts open to see what they're offering us and not just assume that we are the benevolent benefactors and they are the humble recipients.

Giving is part of our dignity as human beings. It might be something like really listening to a five-year-old's insights into a story or accepting a hand with the table clearing from one of the dads. It might be saying 'Yes please' to an offer from a 90-year-old to teach crocheting (while wondering how you explain that they'll need to be CRB cleared...). Perhaps, in Messy Church, we need to build in the opportunity for everyone to give as well as to receive. This is different from demanding. It's a matter of being gracious enough to accept from unlikely people what they have to offer—a cake, a donation of money, an offer to help lead an activity, an idea for next time. Human beings need to feel needed.

The twelve full baskets of leftovers aren't the end of this story about discipleship, according to John. There's a definite narrative thread beyond the actual picnic scene. First, there's a misunderstanding about what sort of king Jesus is. (It's very reassuring that some people get the wrong end of the stick even when Jesus himself is teaching them! We can't expect a 100 per cent success rate ourselves.) The next day, some of them go in search of Jesus again and find him in Capernaum on the other side of the lake. It must have felt more and more like a game of hide and seek. Interestingly, Jesus is in the synagogue now (John 6:59), not out on a hillside. The followers seem rather peeved that he went off without them—'Rabbi, when did you get here?' (John 6:25)—but Jesus, who can see what people are thinking, knows what they're really after. He challenges them about their motivation: 'You're looking for me because you ate all the food you wanted' (v. 26).

Now is the time for bringing out the tough side of being a disciple—when *they* ask leading questions. 'What exactly does God want us to do?' they ask. Jesus replies, 'God wants you to have faith in the one he sent' (vv. 28–29). He starts teaching them about commitment. He pushes these more determined seekers further still, and talks not about picnic rolls but about the bread of life. He takes them beyond the physical and immediate. He talks about his flesh being true food… whoa, this is getting too heavy for some of them. It thins out the followers even more: many of them said, 'This is too hard for anyone to understand' (v. 60), and John writes wryly, 'Because of what Jesus said, many of his disciples turned their backs on him and stopped following him' (v. 66). Jesus is left with the Twelve again.

Look at the context for these seekers, though. They're in a synagogue. The deeper personal questions are being hammered out in a smaller group in an established faith context. Perhaps this is how Messy Church ties up to the established congregation. When people's appetites are whetted by the open-hearted giving and fun of the after-school sessions, some—a few—will be keen to find out more and will find the forum to ask questions within the Alpha courses, the Emmaus courses, the house groups and cell groups of the regular church. The established church must be ready to welcome in the questioners and seekers and give them a place to hammer out answers to their questions.

This may involve a rethink of the established church: after all, is your church a place to come and ask questions or is it a place to sit tidily and absorb what the person at the front is dishing out? If coming to commitment to Jesus is a process that can take several years, as most experts now agree, then there needs to be a place in our church life where individuals can simply experience something of the kingdom in the crowd. But they need to be challenged to move on from there, to put their faith in this Jesus who has fed them. Otherwise they remain crowd members, as many did in Galilee.

How fascinating! Jesus could have added thousands to his following that day on the hillside. He could have been crowned king. Instead, he runs away from the people who want to make him something he's not, he doesn't hide the hard truths from people who ask for them and he ends up with the original twelve disciples. In terms of adding numbers to his group of followers, Jesus is back at square one! But look what he's done: it's been a time of demonstrating God's love and of deepening the faith, understanding and commitment of his true followers. Peter takes a big step of owning his faith in Jesus when he says, 'We have faith in you, and we are sure that you are God's Holy One' (v. 69).

Perhaps Jesus isn't interested in big numbers and short-term effects. Perhaps he's interested in the quality of his followers and the long-term impact of his ministry. Perhaps one of the side-effects of Messy Church will also be a deepening of the faith of the 'home team'.

I would argue that the heavy 'Q&A' session in the synagogue is a step beyond where we're at with the people who come to Messy Church. These are not the committed believers who 'broke bread together' in the early church in Acts 2. Messy Church is a gathering of people who can come and take from God and from the church. They can expect to be fed spiritually and physically. They are given the chance to contribute. They can all meet Jesus. We accept that many will just say 'thanks for a good time' and walk away, some will get the wrong message and some will want to take it further. All of that is absolutely fine. We trust that God will call the people he wants to go further. We'll just provide the fish fingers.

How to reach the messy edges

How did we end up with Messy Church? Why did we feel that this approach might be right for us?

It might be helpful to look at the process we went through to arrive at what is working for us. We had an open meeting for anyone in church who was concerned about children and talked about the needs of the local community, our assets and our limitations. We thought about whether to do something for children only or whether it was more strategic and a better reflection of God's intentions for us to include adults too. We're not organized enough for questionnaires and surveys, but we're very good chatters. We talked to people at the school gate. We walked dogs with them and listened. We talked about it to people in church and out of church and got a gut feeling and vision for what God might be trying to say to us.

We had the buildings, we had the kitchen, we had the artists, we had a wonderful PCC (Church Council) who like to say 'yes'. The rest is messy history… and the messy present… and, by the grace of God, the messy future.

We thought about the lack of 'community feel' and limited ways of making friends, the number of families with children, the difficulties of getting to church on Sundays, the way many parents and carers are keen for children to learn new skills, the need for activities that cost little or nothing, the difficulties of organizing family meals, the mixed blessing of the TV or computer that sucks family members into isolated rooms and non-conversational solitary activity, and the way we all know we ought to do creative things with our children even though it's such an effort, on a school night especially.

We thought about what we would like to see: adults and children coming to worship together, having Bible stories to talk about together, owning their faith, becoming friends with people inside the church and feeling a sense of belonging to the church for themselves.

We took a good look at what resources we have within our church. We decided that our assets include the following:

✣ A surprising number of artistic people: Sonia runs a thriving art class which has grown from one session a week to two with huge waiting lists. She is also a Guider and has done loads with children and youth in the church during her life. Her husband Jim is brilliant with wood. Bob also paints; Louise is a tailor; Vicki can do anything with flowers. Richard has vast armies of Warhammer figures. Lesley, as a childminder, knows all about what art activities are good for child development. Denise has the rare attribute of saying 'Oh, I'll do anything' and meaning it. Catherine and Graham are in Scouts and, with three boys of their own, have lots of ideas for construction-y, science-y activities. And so it goes on. (Incidentally, these people alone range in age from 14 to 70+.)

✣ Lots of good-hearted, Christ-centred people: ours is *not* a furniture-centred church, a church that says, 'But children would spoil the paintwork.' Instead there are people of retirement age and younger who are happy to come and cook, wash up or lead the occasional craft session, and don't mind when the chairs and tables wear out faster than they would do if we never used them. The PCC were delighted to back us financially.

✣ Available people: people who are at home bringing up children or on shift work or retired can be around at the end of school. If we had mainly professional commuting workers who didn't get home until 7pm, we would have had to find another time.

✣ A modern building, with an upper and lower hall, big kitchen and warm comfy church building all under one roof. (Sorry if this sounds like gloating—after a medieval church with no loo, this building is a treat.)

✤ Access to the local Craft Bank with all the card, paper, peculiar-shaped plastic things and other delights you could possibly think of.

Messy Church is a format and focus that works for our area and situation. If we had been a different church, we might have gone down the lines of inventing a sports and games church or photography church or cooking church or singing church. Our main area of available expertise at the moment is in the arts, but every church is different and every area has different needs. Here are some helpful questions that you may wish to consider as you think about what might be right for your situation.

✤ Which group of people are you trying to make church attractive for? Pre-schoolers / children only / whole families / children and after-school carers / single-parent families / tweens / youth / adults only / retired people / a niche interest group / other?
✤ How many are there from this group in your neighbourhood?
✤ How many are known personally by members of the existing church? (People are much more likely to come by personal invitation than 'cold'.)
✤ What is available locally already?
✤ What are the five greatest needs in your local community?
✤ What skills and hobbies do your church members have?
✤ What jobs do they have?
✤ What time of day are they available?
✤ How supportive would your leadership be?
✤ What could your buildings be used for?
✤ How many do they hold comfortably?
✤ What facilities are there in your buildings?
✤ Dream for a moment: what would you love to see?

Think out of the box. Messy Church would work just as well first thing in the morning on a Saturday or Sunday, as a breakfast club for the whole family unit. It might also be manageable just a few times a year, perhaps based round the major Christian festivals. Perhaps the principle of enjoying activities together, rather than either excluding the children or giving all the fun things to the children and leaving adults with the boring grown-up activities, could be put into practice at the Harvest Supper, the Christmas dinner or your patronal festival.

Perhaps a craft-based church is just what you're looking for? Well, do use the ideas in this book as a launch point and to save yourselves from making some of our many mistakes, but please don't follow them slavishly: adapt, throw out bits, invent your own, buy craft books, use the Internet, be creative. We change direction all the time, trying out new ideas, failing miserably, learning constantly. We've included some websites that are good sources of extra ideas after the activities in each unit.

Perhaps, though, the idea of glue and glitter leaves you cold. Read on: if the whole idea is to use a shared interest as a bridge between someone on a messy edge and Jesus at the centre, there are countless ways of being creative that don't go anywhere near a glue pot.

MESSY CHURCH OR...?

Here are some all-age outline suggestions for taking a messy approach to church that don't involve craft and art. It's nowhere near exhaustive, but might spark off inspiration. Some ideas might only have mileage in them for a one-off session; others might run for ages, becoming richer by the year.

If only I could think of a theological justification for a Chocolate Church...

Green Church

Activities could include gardening skills, ecological issues, campaigning for rainforests, visits to gardens, tidying an infirm person's garden.

Green Church could take place in different people's gardens or allotments each month. You could have picnic and praise outdoors, or barbecues. Worship could include a focus on different things you find in gardens: the wonder of a flower, the variety of bugs and beetles, the way a tree grows from a small seed, the disciplines of pruning and weeding. Indoor activities could include flower arranging, potting shed activities, short films on interesting gardens, collages with natural objects, flower pressing, fruit bottling, jam making, cooking with home-grown vegetables, herb drying and so on.

Bible links could include the story of creation and God's care for the world (Genesis 1:1—2:4); the story of Ruth (Ruth), Jonah's vine (Jonah) or Naboth's vineyard (1 Kings 21). In the Gospels there are parables such as the farmer (Matthew 13:1–9), the mustard seed (Matthew 13:31–32) or the vineyard parables (Luke 13:6–9; 20:9–16), Jesus' teaching about the lilies of the field (Matthew 6:28–30), wheat and weeds (Matthew 13:24–30) or the seed falling to the ground (John 12:24). You could use biblical images such as the tree of life (Revelation 22:1–2) and the cross and so on. Seasonal links include harvest festival and Rogationtide.

Sports Church

This theme may be popular as the 2012 Olympics make us all sports-aware. There will probably be government grants available for local sports initiatives. Try contacting Christians in Sport for ideas (www.christiansinsport.org.uk).

Activities could include sports training and playing games, sponsored events to raise money for others and so on. Indoor activities could include table-tennis, snooker, darts, indoor bowls, dance mat, aerobics, line dancing, ceilidh dancing and so on. You could arrange visits to the local swimming pool, sports events, local football matches or ice rink. You could hire films about sporting champions or invite a local dance teacher to help you try out salsa or jive.

Praise could be focused on the idea of being active and the idea of being still. Bible links could include Elijah's sprint ahead of Ahab's chariot (1 Kings 18:41–46), running the race for God (1 Corinthians 9; 2 Timothy 4:7), the image of the church as a body (1 Corinthians 12:12–26), the image of an athlete always pressing on (Hebrews 12:1) or an archer missing the target, like the way we 'fall short of God's perfect standards (Romans 3:23), or rules to play by, like the Ten Commandments (Exodus 20:1–17).

Performing Arts Church

Activities could include drama, dance workshops, specific dance styles, flags, circle dance, drama skills, preparing pieces for worship, or entertaining in old folks' homes, schools, hospitals and similar. You could learn scenery making, backstage skills, costume design, make up and so on. You could arrange visits to shows, video showings or discussions about the themes raised in plays or films.

Worship could include performance and participation drama and dance, experimental services, use of lighting and sound and so on. Bible links could include Miriam dancing (Exodus 15:20), David dancing (2 Samuel 6), the prophets acting out their prophecies (Jeremiah 13:1–11; Jeremiah 19; Ezekiel 12:1–16), the Last Supper (Luke 22:14–20), the Psalms, or the dramatic telling of any story.

Music Church

Activities could include singing, sharing new songs from school or other churches, jamming, practising playing instruments, rhythm, improvising to PowerPoint slide shows, compositions based on stories or pictures, writing and putting on a church musical and so on.

Bible links could include the Psalms, the story of Miriam's tambourine (Exodus 15:20), David's harp (1 Samuel 16:14–23), the last trumpet (1 Corinthians 15:52), the heavenly choirs at Jesus' birth (Luke 2:13–14) and so on. Worship could focus on music and silence.

Photography Church

Activities could include taking and developing photos, digital technology to work on computers with photos and videos, exploring the natural world through photography and film, reflections of God in the world or in people and so on.

Bible links could include the natural world, as found in the Psalms and the Sermon on the Mount (Matthew 5—7), or biblical themes such as mountains, seasides and vines, through the medium of photography. Worship could be very visual with much use of digital projection, film shorts or video clips.

Cookery Church

Activities obviously include cooking and eating, but you could explore foods from different countries and cultures, different food groups, themed foods and different methods of preparing and cooking foods.

Bible links could include food stories, such as the story of Elijah, the ravens and the widow who baked a loaf (1 Kings 17:1–16), the feeding of the five thousand (Luke 9:10–17), the story of manna from heaven (Exodus 16), the parable of the great banquet (Matthew 22:1–14), and food themes such as the feast in Psalm 23. You may find further ideas for linking biblical themes into food in publications such as the *Church Times* cookery column. Worship could be focused on eating together (it's tough but someone's got to do it).

Mechanical Church

Activities could include car maintenance, car washing (for charity), bike maintenance, steam engines, model railways, model aircraft flying, Scalextric, go-kart racing, motocross and so on.

Bible links could include themes of working together (1 Corinthians 12), and the story of God the creator and his attention to detail (Genesis 1:1—2:4; Proverbs 8:22–36). Worship could be very practical, visual and hands-on.

Community Action Church

Activities could include painting graffitied walls, cleaning up playgrounds and ponds, tidying gardens, raising money for charity, raising awareness of causes, organizing trips to events in aid of larger causes, working with your local council on problems in the local community and so on.

Bible links could include the parable of the sheep and goats (Matthew 25:31–46), Jesus' example in caring for outcasts (John 4:1–42; Luke 19:1–10; Mark 1:41–42), and stories that show concern and love for the environment (such as Revelation 8:6—9:21 or Psalm 8). Worship could be about bringing God into the work that you do, using prayer before and after tasks, seeking guidance to keep your eyes open for what God may be saying as you work, placing a focus on love and concern for people in the neighbourhood by praying directly for local people and places and going on prayer walks before and after the work.

CHAPTER 6

Notes on safety and equipment

SAFETY

It is essential that everyone who is involved with the running of Messy Church holds an advanced certificate of disclosure from the Criminal Records Bureau. You will find details of how to apply on the CRB website, www.crb.gov.uk, but you may also find that you can obtain clearance via your PCC, church council, local diocese or church governing body. Alongside CRB checks, we also try to observe good practice for child protection by undertaking a risk assessment of our premises and stipulating that basic safety rules are followed. For example:

✛ Children are not allowed in the kitchen.
✛ The cooks' team has undertaken a food hygiene course.
✛ Hands are washed before cookery activities.

While we try to keep the building as safe and child-friendly as possible, we make it clear that parents and carers are responsible for their children. This is the great joy of having an all-age event rather than one for children only: we are more relaxed as we don't need to keep more than a common-sense eye on the children.

If you're planning a children only event, you'll find useful safety guidelines on the Barnabas website, www.barnabasinchurches.org.uk. Look in the 'Ideas' section under 'A special event or holiday club for children' or 'Organizing a children's event', and in the 'Articles' section under 'Evangelistic children's work: starting an evangelistic children's club'.

Finally, make sure that your craft materials are safe for use with under-fives and that you know exactly what is in the food you are preparing, so that people can make an informed choice with regard to food allergies.

MATERIALS AND EQUIPMENT

We are blessed with a Craft Bank in Portsmouth, where we can get card, bottles, cloth, boxes and all sorts of fantastic stuff for the price of a yearly membership card. If there isn't one in your area, you may need to have a box in church or school and be organized enough to ask for donations of yoghurt pots, wool, ribbons, plastic bottles or other materials well in advance of your next session. It's also worth finding out how to get craft materials through educational suppliers' catalogues, which may be cheaper. For example, try Baker Ross, telephone 0870 458 5440, www.bakerross.co.uk; and S&S Services, telephone 01789 765323, www.ss-services.co.uk. (Be aware that prices in S&S don't include VAT.)

At the start of the year, buy a huge vat of PVA glue, glue spreaders, paintbrushes, ready-mixed paints, washable felt-tips, disposable aprons, waterproof table covers, plain stickers for name badges for each session, decorative stickers, sticky tape, scissors that actually cut (do avoid the horrible children's scissors that merely frustrate the user), packets of googly eyes and so on.

Other useful equipment includes a baby bath, a roll of cleaning cloths and disinfectant spray.

CHAPTER 7

Recipes

Food preparation doesn't need to be complicated or time-consuming, but, if you are slightly more ambitious, you may wish to invest in a basic recipe book such as *Jamie's Dinners: The Essential Cookbook* by Jamie Oliver (Michael Joseph, 2004) to give you more ideas and variety.

The quantities of ingredients for each recipe are hard to estimate, as some small children eat tiny amounts while teenagers might eat loads (and vice versa), but each recipe here makes enough for about ten average servings.

FOOD ALLERGIES

The fact that so many people have food allergies these days might well scare you off cooking for them. Don't let it! Fight the fear! You are a responsible, sensible adult who wouldn't dream of willingly endangering a child or adult and, as such, you have no need to let this uncomfortable question get you down. Remember, all the children have an adult with them and it is their responsibility, not yours, to make sure their child doesn't eat inappropriate foods. Once you start catering for every single allergy that might exist, you'll be left chewing morosely on tofu-flavoured organic rice cakes.

Also, beware the difference between a genuine allergy ('Sidney hyperventilates if he even sees a peanut') and food fads ('Sidney can't eat pasta unless it's got ketchup on it'). Pander to food fads and you'll end up a gibbering wreck. Sorry, but there is no way you can guarantee that the cake Mr Blenkinsop so kindly baked for you has no dairy produce in it. This sounds tough but is only realistic: if someone doesn't know if it's safe or not, it's their decision to eat it or leave it, not yours.

We solve the problem by never cooking anything with actual nuts in, and by having some sort of vegetarian option that matches the rest of the meal (for example, shepherd's pie made with veggie mince or, if we're doing spaghetti bolognese, we might have one panful with meatless tomato sauce), but that is the only general concession we make. We haven't had any other requests for individual catering. Most people are so glad not to have to cook for a night that they'll encourage their children to eat anything we set before them.

MAIN COURSES

Shepherd's pie

The Mayor loved this dish when she visited. If you use lamb, it becomes cottage pie, and if you use veggie mince, it becomes gardener's pie.

✤ Cooking oil for frying
✤ 1kg minced beef, lamb or veggie mince
✤ 2 onions (minced in a food processor so that no one can spot them and wail that they don't like slimy onions)
✤ 1 tbsp garlic purée
✤ 4 carrots, chopped small
✤ 2 pints stock
✤ 2 tbsp dried mixed herbs
✤ 4 tbsp Worcester sauce or HP sauce
✤ 1.5kg potatoes, peeled and cut into equal-sized pieces
✤ 100ml milk

Heat a little oil in a big casserole pan and fry the mince with the onions and garlic purée. Add all the remaining ingredients except the potatoes and milk. Simmer for 45 minutes. Meanwhile, cook the potatoes in plenty of boiling water until tender, then drain and mash, using the milk to help soften and bind them.

Put the mince in a shallow tray and spread the mash over the top. Heat in a hot oven (200°C/400°F/Gas Mark 6) or place under a grill until little brown 'angels' appear on top.

Easy pasta plus

With thanks to Jackie, queen of mince, who has cooked more of the stuff than she cares to remember.

+ 1kg minced beef, lamb or veggie mince
+ Cooking oil for frying
+ 2 jars supermarket Bolognese sauce
+ 1kg pasta
+ 1 bag frozen peas to accompany
+ 1 large block Cheddar cheese (grated)

Fry the mince in a little oil until brown, separating it with a wooden spoon as it cooks. Pour on the sauce and cook for half an hour or according to instructions on jar. Have the boiler on so that you can cook the pasta in boiling water 20 minutes before serving time and the peas 10 minutes before serving time. Put cheese in bowls on tables.

Jacket potatoes

This recipe is the source of Lesley's despair when the oven only cooks the top two potatoes out of fifty!

Cheap time-consuming version: 10 unwashed potatoes that will need scrubbing and pricking.

Expensive easy version: 10 nicely washed potatoes that just need pricking.

For toppings:
✤ 2 tins tuna
✤ 4 tins baked beans
✤ 1 large block Cheddar cheese (grated)
✤ Salad comprising half a cucumber, 1 iceberg lettuce, 2 tomatoes

Lay the potatoes on a baking sheet and place in a hot oven (200°C/400°F/Gas Mark 6). Depending on your oven and the number of potatoes, it's probably best to allow two hours' cooking time, swapping the potatoes round in the oven from top to bottom shelves after an hour.

Roast chicken

This is probably the most expensive of our meals, but sometimes the local supermarket is kind and gives us money off a bulk buy as it's for a good cause.

✤ 2 whole roasting chickens
✤ 1.5kg potatoes (new are easiest)
✤ 1.5kg carrots
✤ Gravy powder or granules
✤ 2 packs of stuffing

Roast the chickens at home in a moderate oven (180°C/350°F/Gas Mark 4) and bring them ready-cooked. New potatoes are the easiest accompaniment, along with carrots. Make a vat of gravy following instructions on the jar. Make stuffing balls: these are less 'school dinnery' than slabs of stuffing. Veggie sausages would make a good alternative for vegetarians.

Ham and wedges

This dish is very easy if your oven gets hot enough. Don't talk to us about idiosyncratic ovens: ours adds an unwelcome element of excitement to the cooking!

+ 10 big potatoes, scrubbed
+ Olive oil
+ 20 small slices ham
+ Salad comprising half a cucumber, 1 iceberg lettuce, 2 tomatoes

Cut the potatoes into wedges—about six per potato. Parboil them for ten minutes, then drain and shake them with a few spoons of olive oil until they're coated. Spread out on baking trays and cook at the top of a very hot oven (210°C/425°F/Gas Mark 7) for at least 40 minutes or until golden. Serve with 2 slices of ham per person, with salad in bowls. Have a cheese option available as a veggie alternative.

Baguette pizza with garlic bread

This recipe is a good one to choose if you only have a grill available. Cook them and keep them somewhere warm until it's time to serve.

+ 2–3 baguettes
+ 1 bottle passata (or pizza topping sauce)
+ Dried herbs
+ 1 large block Cheddar cheese (grated)
+ Optional toppings, such as peppers, pineapple, pepperoni, mushroom, ham and so on
+ Ready-made garlic bread if desired
+ Salad comprising half a cucumber, 1 iceberg lettuce, 2 tomatoes

Cut the baguettes into four and then split them in half lengthwise. Spread on a layer of passata mixed with herbs, sprinkle on cheese and add topping if wanted. Cook in a hot oven (200°C/400°F/Gas Mark 6) or under the grill for 5–10 minutes.

Chicken casserole with hunks of bread

This recipe is cooked on top of the stove, so there's no need to grapple with the vagaries of a temperamental oven.

✢ 1kg chicken pieces, cut small
✢ 3 tbsp plain flour
✢ A little margarine and olive oil
✢ 2 onions, minced
✢ 1 tbsp garlic purée
✢ 2kg carrots, chopped small
✢ 2 pints chicken stock
✢ 2 tbsp mixed herbs
✢ 2 tins chickpeas, if desired
✢ 1 loaf of good-quality bread

Coat the chicken pieces in flour and fry in margarine and oil until golden. Toss the onion, garlic and carrots in the hot oil until slightly soft. Add the stock, herbs and chickpeas (if desired). Simmer for 1 hour. Serve with hunks of good-quality bread. (Quorn pieces cooked in a similar sauce make a good vegetarian alternative.)

Lamb burgers in pitta bread with salad

This dish is oh so easy and so much appreciated by our junk food addicts at the Easter Messy Church tea! Offer veggie burgers as an alternative for vegetarians.

✢ 10 lamb burgers or lamb steaks
✢ 10 pitta pockets
✢ Salad comprising half a cucumber, 1 iceberg lettuce, 2 tomatoes

Cook the burgers as directed and serve in the pitta pockets with salad alongside. For vegetarians, replace the lamb with hummus, hard-boiled egg or fried aubergine slices.

CAKES

There are so many cake recipes out there, it's not worth duplicating them, but we've included a basic fairy cake recipe here, which is useful as a basis for a whole variety of sponge cakes. Just add whatever you fancy to the mix to ring the changes (for example, you could add dried fruit, cocoa powder, coffee flavouring, glacé cherries or lemon juice and zest).

Fairy cakes (makes 20 cakes)

✣ 175g caster sugar
✣ 175g butter (softened) or margarine
✣ 3 eggs (beaten)
✣ 175g self-raising flour

The simplest way to prepare the mixture is to put everything into a food processor and process it until you have a dropping consistency. A handheld whisk works just as well, but go gently to prevent covering everyone and everything in eggs and flour.

Put heaped tablespoons of the mixture into bun cases and bake in the oven at 180°C/350°F/Gas Mark 4 for 15 minutes, or until golden brown and well risen. Cool on a wire rack.

To give you an idea of the variety of cakes that come in every week from our various saintly helpers, we usually have a selection from flapjack, lemon drizzle cake, wrapped chocolate biscuits such as Penguins, iced sponge tray bake, fairy cakes, supermarket buns with homemade icing, Cadbury's chocolate logs, chocolate cake, Jammy Dodgers, buttered fruit loaf, Jaffa Cakes, fruit scones... and so on.

Yes, it's *very* nice.

While we're on the food front, don't forget to buy squash, milk, tea, coffee, sugar and biscuits for arrival time as well. If you have access to a bulk wholesale outlet or cash and carry store, such as Costco, this would give excellent value for money. You can locate your nearest store on their website at www.costco.com.

CHAPTER 8

Introduction to thematic programmes

The themes in the following sections will give you some ideas for series that last about a term each. By the time you've been through a few of these, I hope you'll be itching to try out your own ideas. It's worth looking for inspiration for new series in Barnabas books and other publications. For example, you might want to follow a complete book of stories, such as *Stories to Read Aloud* (Patrick Coghlan, BRF, 2004), or think about using parables, or biblical themes such as journeys, animals, heroes or villains. The possibilities are as vast as your imagination!

SETTING THE SCENE

Each Messy Church session has a clear theme and every aspect of Messy Church can be used to reinforce this theme. Reinforcement through a variety of media is good educational practice and will help everyone to remember what they experience and learn.

In the welcome time, you could include colouring sheets or word-searches linked with the theme. As you welcome everyone briefly, you can announce what the theme is: 'Today we're thinking about mountains! I wonder how many stories about mountains you'll discover as you do your crafts.' Or you may challenge everyone to discover the theme for themselves: 'Today we're exploring a brilliant story Jesus told. I wonder how long it will take you to discover what that story is!'

Of course, the crafts relate closely, or (when we're desperate) tangentially, to the theme. The celebration in your worship space can include visual reminders (props, pictures, a focal point) as well as the content of the service itself. Even the food can be linked to the theme occasionally: lamb at Easter time, fish fingers for the feeding of the five thousand. If you have a spare person who could take digital photos of the craft creations as they are being made, these could be quickly downloaded on to a laptop and projected at the start of the service, perhaps even referred to during the service itself.

(An aside about photography: you may choose to be well-organized and ask adults to fill in permission slips for the children to be filmed. We decided that it would be too difficult to stay up to date, with newcomers every week, so we settled for taking photos of the crafts rather than the children. If you're in any doubt about what is best practice, please consult your Child Protection Officer.)

You'll have a team of helpers, each leading a craft activity. Some of these helpers will find that they chat about spiritual matters quite naturally and easily; others will find it deeply embarrassing. But valuable truths will be communicated through conversations over a paint pot as well as from the front in the main worship session. To give everyone a hand with knowing what to talk about as they lead their activity, we've supplied a suggestion with each craft activity for talking about the bigger subject. This should give leaders a conversation starter and will help them not to repeat the same story over and over again at the different craft points. For example, in the session on 'mountains', one craft activity encourages the leader to talk about the feeding of the five thousand, another about God's holy mountain from Isaiah and another about Elijah on Mount Carmel. Sometimes the subjects are biblical, sometimes they encourage everyone to express their own experiences and opinions, and sometimes they are to wonder at the marvels of creation or science.

If you only have one copy of this book, you'll need to copy down the 'Talk about' subject for each helper and try to allow a few minutes to check with them that they are happy about that subject. Sometimes even our keenest helpers can be a little hazy about a Bible story and may need reminding.

PREPARING THE WORSHIP SPACE

We're very blessed with the building we have: we can take people away from the craft tables and into church merely by walking from one room to another. This gives us a change of focus, but doesn't risk losing stragglers along the way or making for a mass 'Where's my coat?' hunt. If you are doing Messy Church in a different situation, it's worth thinking imaginatively about the best setting for worship.

If you do have the facilities to hold the worship in a separate room, this could be a practical help to the cooks' team, as they can get on with setting the tables and putting out dishes of food without feeling that they're distracting from the celebration. The smell of food can be a distraction too!

It sounds ironic, but is your church the best place to worship? Some churches are so cold and uncomfortable that relaxed worship is difficult through layers of parkas and duffel coats, and between pews designed for adults. There is certainly a case for using a building where Christians may have worshipped for centuries—and for helping people on the fringe to feel that a church building is theirs, too. Think carefully about where is best for what you're trying to achieve. If you want to use the church building for your worship space, but you have to leave the craft space in order to do so, make sure everyone is safe and supervised as they move from one space to another. Could you move in formal procession so that you all arrive together instead of in dribs and drabs? Will it be warm or cold when you get there? Is it dark and scary (or is that mysterious and atmospheric...) or welcoming?

If you only have one room at your disposal for craft, food and worship, consider this as an opportunity rather than a problem. After all, it's lovely to be creative, worship and eat all in the same room: what a marvellous statement about the way God is working in our everyday lives as well as being a holy 'other' God! Of course, though, it presents practical issues. You may want to think about 'zoning' your space. A good principle is that people need to have boundaries between different spaces and need to move *from* a messy craft space *into* a calm / exciting / atmospheric / mysterious / intriguing (or however you plan it to be) worship space. It can be a space in the same room, but it is a different 'set aside' space. This will help everyone to know what behaviour is acceptable in the different spaces.

Could you divide up the room using tape on the floor or using screens, chairs or tables? Could you roll out a large rug to sit on? Perhaps a circle of chairs could be set up. Could the space be made attractive with a candle, focal table or cross? Might everyone hear something intriguing as they come into it: music, bells, a sound that echoes the day's theme, a chant or song to join in with? Is there something that could be passed round or touched—a tray of sand to run your fingers through, a bowl of water to dip your hand in or a beautiful piece of fabric, a picture postcard or something from the natural world to pass round? Your numbers will determine what you set up. Might everyone remove their shoes before they enter? (It's worth remembering that for small children and older people who find it hard to bend, this could be a major undertaking. There is also the teenage boy sock odour issue to consider.)

Look at your space creatively. This is your chance to devise a church structure. Do you want to have echoes of the Sunday worship structure or of the structure of collective worship that the children are used to in school, or do you want to help them experience something completely new? Do you love the ordered shape of people sitting in rows of pews or do you long for a looser, more informal structure? Do you think a circle of seats expresses the unity of a church or is a half-circle better for visibility? Could you mark out the shape of a cross and sit within that? Try out some different ideas: you could be changing the face of church as we know it!

Do listen to suggestions from all ages as you evolve your own unique style of worship for this new congregation. Perhaps you hadn't realized that everything is invisible to those who are only three feet tall unless they're in the front row. Maybe you didn't know how hideously uncomfortable the chairs are if your legs are short or long, or if you have back problems. Maybe you hadn't noticed the layer of dead beetles on the floor that you expect the toddlers to sit on, or the sinister floor-level smell in a corner of the room... Remember, this congregation is new wine and might burst your old wineskins.

Web help

For craft ideas and resources, try a web search. For example, for the first unit, 'Abraham and Sarah', you could search *Christian craft stars*, *Christian craft sand* or *Craft Abraham* (without quotation marks). Alternatively, see the Messy Church website www.messychurch.org.uk for other sites that you might find useful.

God's family, our family

Old Testament stories about families

UNIT 1

Abraham and Sarah

AIM

To see that we all belong to the same family of believers, which started with the story of Abraham and Sarah and God's promise to them.

BIBLE BACKGROUND (Genesis 12—21)

This is a huge, epic story but we've simplified it down to a few elements. God calls Abram to go on a journey with him. His wife Sarai can't have children and this makes them very sad. On the journey, God promises Abram that he will have more children than there are stars in the sky or grains of sand in the desert. As a sign of that promise, God changes Abram's name to Abraham and Sarai's name to Sarah.

God's promise comes true when Sarah finally does have a baby, called Isaac, when she's very old. The great-great-great-(lots of greats)-grandchildren of this family are the members of God's family here today, so we are all members of the same family—God's family of believers. God's promise starts with small things but can become incredibly massive.

FOOD

Pasta plus

Serve up the pasta and peas from the kitchen. Have bowls of sauce and bowls of grated cheese on the tables to be dished up there by parents or teenagers. It takes too long to put everything on a plate in the kitchen and to get it out to people hot.

ACTIVITIES

Printing stars

You will need: Craft sponges (from Early Learning Centre or similar), waxy potatoes (washed and dried), pots of poster paint in different colours, dark paper or card

Use the sponges or potatoes cut into star shapes with at least three colours of paint. Print the stars on to dark paper or card.

Talk about
During this activity, talk about how many stars you can see in the night sky and encourage everyone to count them tonight.

'Sand' bottles

You will need: A variety of different-coloured beads or coloured 'sands' made from salt and powder poster paint (see below), clear plastic bottles

Use a variety of different-coloured beads or coloured 'sands' to fill clear plastic bottles with layers of different colours. Seal them tightly!

You can make 'sand' with salt and poster paint. For sand colour, add a teaspoon of yellow and half a teaspoon of red paint to a 1 kg bag of salt.

Talk about

During this activity, talk about counting the grains of sand in the bottles and how the numbers just go on and on. Ask what the biggest number is that they can think of. Marvel together at the idea of infinity.

Family cards

> **You will need**: Mediumweight white or coloured card, stickers, punches, coloured scraps and so on, PVA glue, scissors, coloured pens or pencils

Design a card to give to someone you love in your family, maybe living near you or maybe far away. Use stickers, punches and coloured scraps to make it look beautiful.

Talk about

Talk about the way families go back and back and back in time, from parents to grandparents and great-grandparents to even further back. Expect to hear lots about elderly relatives! Talk about how one day the children might be parents or grandparents or great-grandparents themselves! Family stretches out across time.

Warhammer workshop

> **You will need**: Warhammer models (encourage the children to bring in their collections), enamel paints in different colours, small brushes, jars of cleaner, kitchen paper

Have fun painting the models together!

Talk about
Talk about the fun of collecting things, looking after our collections and seeing them grow.

Watercolour faces

> **You will need:** Watercolour paints in different colours, water-colour paper, paintbrushes, jars of clean water, kitchen paper

Use watercolours to paint a face on a small piece of watercolour paper.

Talk about
Talk about the different colours that go into making the whole picture, just like different people go into making up a whole family.

Journeys

> **You will need:** Prepared outlines of cars, trains, camels, horses and caravans (drawn in thick marker pen on paper), poster paints in different colours, paint brushes, jars of clean water, kitchen paper

Using your prepared outlines, invite everyone to paint their family on a journey using one of these means of transport. Encourage them to add extended family, church family and friends.

Talk about
Talk about journeys that families have to make sometimes. Has anyone made a journey with his or her family recently? How was it? How did they manage when they all wanted to go in different directions?

Star mobiles

You will need: Cardboard star shapes, glitter and glitter glue, shiny gift ribbon, wire coathangers

Decorate cardboard star shapes with glitter and glitter glue, and hang them on shiny gift ribbon from a wire coathanger.

Talk about
Talk about the stars in the sky that are there even in the day when we can't see them. Each one of them is different.

Star sticking

You will need: Sheets of dark paper, tubes of shiny silver stars, PVA glue, silver or gold pens

On dark paper, use shiny silver stars to create your own constellation, and give it a name.

Talk about
Talk about the patterns the stars make in the sky and how people have seen animals, birds and heroes in the constellations.

Sand tray

You will need: A sandpit or sandtray filled with silver sand, seaside buckets, scoops and spoons

Have a sandpit or sandtray to play in, with buckets, scoops and spoons.

Talk about

Talk about the desert and how it's always changing as the wind blows on it. Talk about the seaside and making sandcastles and sandpies.

Ziggurat sandwiches

> **You will need:** Slices of thin white bread, various sandwich fillings, table knives, paper plates

Have slices of thin white bread, ready cut into different-sized squares, and various sandwich fillings: jam, cheese, ham, yeast extract, lettuce, chocolate spread, sandwich spread and so on. Make ziggurats by sandwiching the squares of bread together in ever-decreasing sizes with different fillings until you have made a pyramid-shaped edifice. You may or may not want to eat it...

Talk about

Talk about the ancient city of Ur, where people worshipped nature gods in buildings called ziggurats, and how Abraham met the true God not in a building but out in the desert.

CELEBRATION

Setting up the church or worship space

> **You will need:** Large cardboard stars, PowerPoint loaded with digital pictures of finished artwork (optional), samples of artwork from each activity station, small bowl of silver sand

Put large cardboard stars out on the floor and hang more wherever possible. If you are using PowerPoint, have this ready to display photos of artwork as everyone comes in.

Song selection

I reach up high (*Kidsource 1*, 171)
Any kind of weather (Doug Horley, *Humungous Song Book*, 2)
Faith as small as a mustard seed (Doug Horley, *Humungous Song Book*, 15)
Have we made our God too small? (Doug Horley, *Humungous Song Book*, 23)

Talk

Looking at the artwork, I see lots of sand and lots of stars. It reminds me of a story.

Use pictures loaded into PowerPoint or samples of artwork from each activity station to tell the story.

There was a man called Abraham. He was very old and he was married to Sarah. They were very sad because they had no children.

But one night, out in the desert, God made Abraham a special promise. God said to Abraham, 'Look up and count the stars—if you can. That's how many people there will be in your family one day...'

Show PowerPoint image or artwork sample of stars.

'... Think of the sand on the seashore. How many grains can you count?

I'll bless you and give you such a large family that one day they'll be as many as the stars in the sky or the grains of sand on the seashore.'

Pick up the bowl of sand and let the sand run through your fingers into the bowl.

God kept his promise. We're Abraham's family, because we're God's family—the Christian family of faith. We've millions of brothers and sisters of all ages and colours in every land all over the world.

Prayer response

Encourage everyone to think of something to thank God for. Ask them to put up their hand to say what that thing is. As people give their response, repeat it and invite everyone to say, 'Lord God, we thank you.'

Final blessing

Lord, thank you that we are one big family of your people throughout the world and throughout history. Help us to live as one family, loving each other through thick and thin. Amen

Messy Grace

May the grace of our Lord Jesus Christ (*Hold out your hands as if expecting a present*)
And the love of God (*Put your hands on your heart*)
And the fellowship of the Holy Spirit (*Hold hands*)
Be with us all now and for ever. Amen! (*Raise hands together on the word 'Amen'*)

UNIT 2

Joseph

AIM

To become familiar with the story of Joseph, to discover more about trusting God in bad times, to think about family quarrels and to explore the theme of God's rescue.

BIBLE BACKGROUND (Genesis 37—50)

The story of Joseph is really rich. A lot of the component parts should come out in the craft activities, so that in the celebration the story can be reinforced and told with, rather than to, those present. Remember to keep bringing the characters to life for the children and adults so that they see the links between this ancient story and their own lives. For example, you might say, 'I wonder if you've ever been jealous of your brother or sister? I wonder if you have felt so cross with someone that you felt like killing them? Have you ever wondered what God's plan for your life could be? Have you ever felt that God has deserted you?' and so on.

FOOD

Jacket potatoes

Serve the potatoes from the kitchen. Have salad, cheese, beans and tuna in bowls on the tables for everyone to help themselves. (Beans and cheese are very popular, tuna less so.)

ACTIVITIES

Dream pictures

You will need: Washing-up liquid, poster paint in different colours, wide shallow dishes, drinking straws, sheets of paper, smaller squares of paper, PVA glue

Mix washing-up liquid with poster paint in wide shallow dishes. Blow through a straw into the mixture to make it frothy and then place a sheet of paper gently over the top to print the bubble pattern. On a smaller square of paper, draw your dream and then glue the dream picture on to the bubble print so that the bubble print forms a frame for the dream.

Talk about

Talk about dreams, how God can talk to people through dreams and how most of us have a dream for our life. We might find that as we follow our dream, God has very different plans for us that are even better than our dream.

Big coloured coat

You will need: The outline of a very simple coat drawn on a large piece of card, strips of ribbon or material, PVA glue

Invite everyone to choose some strips of ribbon or material and glue them on to the outline of a coat to make it look beautiful.

Talk about

Talk about the beautiful coat that Jacob gave to Joseph as a present. Ask everyone what is their favourite piece of clothing at the moment.

Coat design collage

> **You will need**: A cardboard template of a coat, felt-tipped pens, scraps of material, scissors, buttons and sequins, safety pins (optional), needle and thread (optional), small pieces of card (optional), PVA glue

Have the cardboard template of a coat to draw round with felt-tipped pens on to a piece of material. (You might want to have a tiny template for older people and a larger template for younger people.) Cut out the coat shape, decorate with buttons and sequins (either glued or sewn on) and either turn it into a badge, using a safety pin sewn on to the back, or glue on to a piece of card as a picture.

Talk about
Talk about the musical *Joseph and the Amazing Technicolour Dreamcoat*.

Gift box decoration

> **You will need**: Small gift boxes, scraps of fabric, buttons, sequins or basic embroidery materials, wrapped sweets (not hard-boiled, due to choking hazard)

Decorate small gift boxes using fabric, buttons, sequins or basic embroidery. Use a heart or cross motif as a symbol of love. Put a wrapped sweet inside and encourage the idea of giving the present away to show how much you love someone.

Talk about
Talk about presents from friends or members of your family, and how you might want to give your family or friends a present just because you love them so much.

Loaves of bread

You will need: Ready-made bread dough, greaseproof paper, pencils, baking trays, egg yolk or milk (optional: beware of food allergies), pastry brush (optional)

Have some bread dough cut into strips. Give each person three strips, to be braided into a plaited roll. Place on a piece of greaseproof paper with their name on it. Glaze with egg yolk or milk if desired, and bake in a very hot oven (200°C/400°F/Gas Mark 6) for 15–20 minutes, until golden brown.

Talk about

Remind everyone of the baker in prison who had a dream about bread rolls (Genesis 40:1–23).

Thumbprint people

You will need: Poster paint in different colours, sheets of paper, felt-tipped pens

Make twelve thumbprints in poster paint. When they're dry, decorate them with felt-tipped eyes, mouths, beards and clothes to be Joseph and his eleven brothers.

Talk about

Talk about the way very different people make up a family and how hard it can be to live together when you feel very different from them. Talk about ways of getting on with each other that you have found helpful.

Needlecase embroidery

You will need: Small rectangles of felt, basic embroidery materials, buttons or sequins, PVA glue, embroidery needles (beware of hazards with very young children)

Use a small rectangle of felt as the cover. Decorate the front of the needlecase with a few embroidery stitches or by sewing on buttons or sequins. Younger people may need to glue the decorations on. Older people may want to learn a style of stitching and embroider an initial. Cut a slightly smaller piece of felt and sew it on to the cover piece, using running stitch down the 'spine'. Fold in half and press to make a needlebook. Add one needle to start off the collection.

Talk about
Talk about what equipment you need to sew with, and what you can make with cloth.

Watercolour painting

You will need: Watercolour paints, sheets of paper, brushes, jars of clean water, kitchen paper

Use bright colours in stripes to design a coat for Joseph. Which colours go well together?

Talk about
Talk about the brightest-coloured clothes you've ever seen. Show some pictures of clothes with very unusual designs and colours from a designer such as Zandra Rhodes.

False beards

> **You will need:** Scraps of fur fabrics, scraps of dark brown and black fabrics, scissors, dark wool and a darning needle, ribbon (optional)

Using your selection of fur fabrics and dark brown and black fabrics, cut out a triangle big enough to fit on to the chin as a beard. Cut a mouth hole so that it comprises a moustache and beard. Using dark wool in a darning needle, sew on a piece of wool or ribbon at each side that can be tied behind the head to hold the beard in place. You might have to do the sewing for younger people. Wear your beard with pride!

Talk about
Talk about the 'hairy Ishmaelites' who took Joseph off to Egypt and sold him as a slave (Genesis 37:25–28).

Camel ornaments

> **You will need:** Metallic wax crayons, a selection of coins, soft-leaded pencils, PVA glue, sheets of paper, scissors, pieces of thin card, a hole punch, shiny ribbon or strong thread, laminating machine (optional)

Using metallic wax crayons, make rubbings of coins on to paper. Cut them out carefully and glue them on to thin card so that there is one rubbing on each side. If possible, laminate the coin. Holepunch it and thread a shiny ribbon or strong thread through it to make a hanging ornament for your camel (or car... or scooter).

Talk about

Talk about the way Joseph was sold for 20 pieces of silver and whisked away from his family on a camel. Camels were decorated with gold ornaments, rather like we might have soft toys dangling from our car mirrors.

CELEBRATION

Setting up the church or worship space

> **You will need**: Brightly coloured jumpers or jackets, coat-hangers, toy camels or pictures of the pyramids, PowerPoint loaded with digital pictures of finished artwork (optional), samples of artwork from each activity station, a large box or bag (for the talk) containing, a bright coat or robe, a small knife, a small loaf of bread and a picture of a smiling face.

Decorate the worship space with brightly coloured jumpers or jackets hanging on coathangers, and toy camels or pictures of the pyramids. If you are using PowerPoint, have this ready to display photos of artwork as everyone comes in.

Song selection

Our God is a great big God (*Great Big God* CD, Vineyard)
Great Great Brill Brill (Doug Horley, *Humungous Song Book*, 66)
Every move I make (Integrity Music *Shout to the Lord Kids*, 1)
Father God I wonder (*Kidsource 1*, 52)

Talk

Link the crafts and decorations to Joseph. For each part of this story, where indicated, bring an object out of a large box or bag.

Joseph had eleven brothers. Maybe you sometimes quarrel with your brother or sister. Well, Joseph and his brothers often quarrelled, partly because Joseph's brothers were jealous of the beautiful coat that their dad, Jacob, had given to Joseph.

Bring a bright coat or robe out of the box or bag.

Also, Joseph had dreams they didn't like. For example, he dreamed that the sun, the moon and eleven stars were bowing down to him. His brothers thought he was showing off.

So the brothers plotted to kill Joseph. They threw him down a dry well, but then, instead of killing him, they decided to sell him to some slave traders who were passing by. The traders took Joseph to Egypt while the brothers daubed the beautiful coat with the blood of a goat and told their dad that Joseph had been killed by a wild animal.

Bring a small knife out of the box or bag.

In Egypt, Joseph was sold as a slave and, although he was very hardworking, he was thrown in jail for something he didn't do. While he was in prison, he told some prisoners what their dreams meant, and later he told Pharaoh what his dream meant. The harvests would fail and there was going to be a famine, so Egypt would have to stock up on food.

Bring a small loaf of bread out of the box or bag.

The famine came to the whole area—and Egypt was the only place with food, thanks to Joseph. Joseph's brothers came to Egypt to buy food, but they didn't recognize Joseph. What would Joseph do? Should he get his revenge on them for being so mean all those years ago?

No! He told them who he was and forgave them. 'Even though you meant to harm me, God made it all turn out well so that everyone would be saved,' he said. So they brought Jacob, their father, to Egypt and God reunited them all.

Bring a picture of a smiling face out of the box or bag.

God can take things that go wrong and mend them and turn them to good. He wants to bring us together as his Christian family.

Prayer response

Think of someone you've quarrelled with recently. Let's say sorry to God and ask him to help us forgive them and to make up.

Leader: Thank you, Lord God, that, despite our mistakes, you can make things turn out for good.

All: Lord God, we thank you.

Leader: Thank you for Messy Church and all our friends and family here.

All: Lord God, we thank you.

Leader: Thank you for our families and homes, our brothers and sisters and those who love us.

All: Lord God, we thank you.

Leader: Thank you for our friends at church and school.

All: Lord God, we thank you.

Final blessing

Lord, thank you that we are one big family of your people throughout the world and throughout history. Help us to live as one family, loving each other through thick and thin. Amen

Messy Grace

May the grace of our Lord Jesus Christ (*Hold out your hands as if expecting a present*)
And the love of God (*Put your hands on your heart*)
And the fellowship of the Holy Spirit (*Hold hands*)
Be with us all now and for ever. Amen! (*Raise hands together on the word 'Amen'*)

Moses

AIM

To tell the story of Moses and explore the theme of God's rescue.

BIBLE BACKGROUND (Exodus 1—15)

There are plenty of stories about Moses up to and including the escape from Egypt, so the theme follows the story up to that point and doesn't include the stories about the years in the desert or the giving of the Ten Commandments. The links with our lives might lie in questions of being bullied, feeling inadequate for a job, trusting God in difficult times and trusting that God has a plan for our lives.

FOOD

Roast chicken

Such an important celebration story needs a festive meal. If you so wish, you could do the Passover meal here instead, as it would fit well (see page 159), but we saved it until Easter.

Serve up chicken portions and stuffing from the kitchen. Have gravy, potatoes and carrots on the tables.

ACTIVITIES

Pyramid construction

You will need: Cocktail sticks, dried peas

See what 3D shapes you can construct out of cocktail sticks with a pea at every angle to stick them together.

Talk about
Talk about God's people having to make bricks out of straw and mud for Pharaoh's pyramids.

Mud pies

You will need: Sterilized garden mud (see below), self-hardening clay (optional)

Well in advance, sterilize some garden mud by boiling it up with water in an old saucepan and allow it to cool. Alternatively, you could use clay. Play with it. Possibly outside.

Talk about
Talk about God's people working in the scorching heat, making bricks for the pyramids.

Papyrus weaving

You will need: Sheets of A4 paper, scissors, PVA glue

Cut an A4 piece of paper into strips lengthways, leaving the far end of the paper uncut so that the strips form a kind of fringe. Cut another piece similarly, but widthways. Thread the strips in and out of each other to make a woven pattern. Glue to secure.

Talk about
Talk about how Egyptians made paper to write on by weaving papyrus leaves.

Hieroglyphics

You will need: Examples of Egyptian hieroglyphs, sheets of paper, pencils, thin brushes, black paint, jars of clean water, kitchen paper

Look at some examples of hieroglyphs and their meanings. Draw your own with pencil, then make them look Egyptian by using thin brushes and black paint to paint over them.

Talk about
Talk about how only a very few people used to be able to read and write. In Egypt, the scribes wrote everything down in hieroglyphics (picture writing).

Plague picture

You will need: Pictures of the ten plagues (see Exodus 7:14— 9:6), sheets of beige paper or card, felt-tipped pens, PVA glue

Photocopy the plague pictures. Stick them on a sheet of beige paper or card to look like Egyptian wall paintings. Decorate the borders with felt-tipped pens.

Talk about

Talk about the way all of Egypt suffered because their king was so stubborn.

DIY boils

You will need: Fake wounds (see below), make-up and adhesive (beware of skin allergies), tissue paper in various colours (see below)

Using joke-shop or theatrical suppliers' fake wounds, make-up and adhesive, design and stick on your own suppurating boil. A cheaper, more temporary version can be made with white, pink, orange, yellow and red tissue paper papier mâché.

Talk about

Talk about how horrible it feels to have chicken pox or a big spot.

Origami frogs

You will need: Sheets of A4 paper, pencils, scissors

See www.enchantedlearning.com/crafts/origami/frog for instructions.

Talk about

Talk about what one frog in the garden is like, then what it might be like to have frogs everywhere—in your bed, in your kitchen, in your toilet.

Stinky smells

> **You will need:** A variety of smelly items (see below), small jars with screw-on lids

Make a collection of things that smell disgusting—for example, bad egg, mouldy cheese, rotting banana, damp dishcloth gone mouldy. Put each substance in an opaque sealed pot and guess what they are by giving each person a brief sniff of each.

Talk about

Talk about how horrible Egypt must have smelt after the ten plagues.

Reed Sea collage

> **You will need:** Lining wallpaper (unpasted), felt-tipped pens, blue cellophane or wrapping paper, sheets of A4 paper, scraps of coloured or holographic paper, scissors, PVA glue

On the lining wallpaper, draw a picture of Moses and the Israelites crossing the Reed Sea. Add blue cellophane or wrapping paper waves. Design weird and wonderful fish to stick in the sea on either side of the path.

Talk about

Talk about times when you've been rescued from a dangerous situation and listen to stories about times when other people have been rescued.

Flat bread

You will need:
- ✢ 225g plain flour
- ✢ 1 tsp salt
- ✢ 150ml cold water
- ✢ Baking tray
- ✢ Greaseproof paper
- ✢ Fork
- ✢ Cooking oil (to grease the paper)

Combine the dry ingredients with the water to make a dough. Knead the dough for about ten minutes. Flatten it out and perforate it in a pattern with a fork. Place on greaseproof paper with your name on. Bake in a moderate oven (180°C/350°F/Gas Mark 4) for 10–15 minutes.

Talk about
Talk about how bread usually takes time to rise, but that if you need it quickly, you can make flat bread without yeast. This is what Moses told the Israelites to do when they had to escape from Egypt in a hurry.

CELEBRATION

Setting up the church or worship space

You will need: Two long blue cloths, palm tree made from a cardboard tube and paper leaves, paper and pen for every person, PowerPoint loaded with digital pictures of finished artwork (optional), samples of artwork from each activity station

Decorate the worship space by spreading two long blue cloths down the nave or central passageway. Place a palm tree at the front. Have a piece of paper and pen for every person. If you are using PowerPoint, have this ready to display photos of artwork as everyone comes in. Comment on the artwork.

Song selection

O Lord you're so great (*Kidsource 1*, 270)
We are marching (*Kidsource 1*, 350)
It's excellent to be obedient (*Kidsource 1*, 346)
Give thanks to the Lord our God and King (Integrity Music, *Shout to the Lord Kids 1* CD or *Songs of Fellowship 3*, 1241)
King of love (Doug Horley, *Humungous Song Book*, 50)

Talk

Get everyone to come out and join in the action with you. Act it out as you go along. Use the blue cloths as the sea, lifting them up to make two walls of water. One person could play Moses, one Pharaoh and some of them could be the Egyptians.

We were so miserable. We were slaves in Egypt. We had to mix mud and straw to make bricks in the scorching sun. Pharaoh's soldiers beat us if we didn't work hard enough. We cried to God for help:

Shout: 'Save us, Lord!'

When the time was right, God sent his friend Moses to rescue us. Moses went to Pharaoh and said, 'Let my people go.' But Pharaoh said 'No.'

Moses said, 'If you don't let my people go, terrible things will happen.' But still Pharaoh said, 'No.'

The terrible things did happen to the Egyptians. The River Nile turned to blood. There were frogs, gnats and flies.

Mime the attacks of these plagues.

But when Moses went to Pharaoh and said, 'Let my people go', Pharaoh still said 'No.'

All the animals died; there were horrible boils and hailstorms.

Mime the attacks of these plagues.

But when Moses went to Pharaoh and said, 'Let my people go', Pharaoh still said 'No.'

There were locusts and darkness.

Mime the attacks of these plagues.

But when Moses went to Pharaoh and said, 'Let my people go', Pharaoh still said 'No.'

Then the most terrible thing happened. Moses got us ready. 'Get ready for a long journey. There isn't time to let your bread rise, so bake it without yeast. Kill a lamb and paint its blood round your door. Then when the angel of death comes, it will know not to come in, and it will pass over your house and you will be safe.'

Mime painting round a doorway.

We did as Moses said, and God kept us safe. But the Egyptians weren't. In every house, the oldest boy died. So Pharaoh told Moses, 'Go!'

We went out of Egypt as far as the shores of the Reed Sea.

Mime walking.

But Pharaoh changed his mind and galloped after us with his army in speedy chariots.

Mime galloping in chariots.

Moses prayed to God and stretched out his stick over the sea. The sea parted and we went through on a dry path. When we were all safely across, Moses stretched out his stick again and the Egyptians who were chasing after us were swept away in the water.

Act this out by drawing the cloths over the Egyptians.

So, thanks to God, we were safe and free at last.

Mime partying.

Prayer response

Write or draw on your paper one thing that you are worried about or scared of that you want to bring to God. Place it in the gap between the cloths of the sea. When they are all there, draw the cloths over the pieces of paper.

Final blessing

Thank you, Lord, that you want us to be free of the things that worry and scare us. We pray that you will help us to remember that you are stronger than any of these worries and fears. Amen

Messy Grace

May the grace of our Lord Jesus Christ (*Hold out your hands as if expecting a present*)
And the love of God (*Put your hands on your heart*)
And the fellowship of the Holy Spirit (*Hold hands*)
Be with us all now and for ever. Amen! (*Raise hands together on the word 'Amen'*)

UNIT 4

Joshua

AIM

To enjoy the story of Joshua and the battle of Jericho and to pick up on the theme of 'nothing is impossible for God'.

BIBLE BACKGROUND (Joshua 6)

The Israelites were coming into the promised land and needed to conquer the fortress city of Jericho. It seemed impossible, but with God's help they overcame this obstacle. God can help us with apparently insurmountable problems in our lives if we are obedient to him and are ready to do anything he asks—however surprising.

FOOD

Sausage and mash with peas or beans

Serve sausage and mash from the kitchen and have plates of vegetables on the tables. Walk round with the ketchup bottle, rationing it. For vegetarians, offer veggie sausages as an alternative.

ACTIVITIES

Texture pictures

> **You will need**: A simple picture of a walled city, ideally in the Holy Land, gravel, sand and small pebbles, PVA glue

Copy the picture on to thick card or thin wood. Fill each area with glue, then pour on gravel, sand and pebbles in turn to fill in the different parts of the picture.

Talk about
Talk about how strong stone is as a building material.

Graffiti wall

> **You will need**: A4 orange sugar paper, colouring pencils, felt-tipped pens, lining wallpaper (unpasted, to use as backing paper), PVA glue

Decorate an A4 piece of orange sugar paper to be a brick with your name and your own design. Glue the finished bricks on to a backing sheet in a wall pattern. Alternatively, make up a brick wall with a large sheet of backing paper and invite everyone to come and graffiti words and doodles on it with felt-tipped pens.

Talk about
Talk about how walls can be made up of stones or bricks. Look at the different patterns of bricks in walls round about you.

Flower arranging

You will need: Cubes of oasis (flower arrangers' foam), masking tape, plastic saucers, artificial or real flowers

Tape cubes of oasis into a plastic saucer (the sort that you use under a flowerpot) and build up an arrangement from artificial or real flowers.

Talk about
Talk about the promised land—a wonderful place where God wanted his people to live. No doubt there were flowers all over it.

Edible stones

You will need: Ready-made fondant icing, coffee essence or brown food colouring, chocolate sprinkles and icing sugar, bun cases

Make up fondant icing with some coffee essence or brown food colouring. Have some chocolate sprinkles and icing sugar for 'brick dust'. Make up irregular-shaped stones and put in bun cases to take home.

Talk about
Talk about the way every stone in the world is different from every other stone. God's creation is amazingly varied. Although it's not a good idea to put stones in your mouth, these are going to be edible ones, so you can.

Stone painting

You will need: Stones (from a garden centre), poster paint in different colours, brushes, jars of clean water, clear varnish (optional)

Buy stones from the garden centre and paint them with poster paints. Varnish if desired, although there may not be time for the varnish to set.

Talk about
Talk about the durability and lasting qualities of stones.

Musical instruments: shakers

You will need: Dried peas, rice or small stones, lidded tubes, boxes and bottles, coloured sticky tape, crêpe paper, stickers and gift ribbon

Place a few dried peas, rice or stones in tubes, boxes and bottles, sealing the lids tightly with coloured tape. Decorate with strips of crêpe paper, stickers and gift ribbon.

Talk about
Talk about music and how music makes you feel.

Musical instruments: tambourines

You will need: Circles of strong card, strong ribbon or string, small hard objects (see below), hole punch or pair of compasses

Using a dinner plate as a template, cut circles of strong card, or use plastic party plates as the base. Using strong ribbon or string, thread small hard objects, especially metallic ones, together loosely. Punch holes around the circular base and tie the objects on to it. Cotton reels, bolts, washers or bottle tops ready punched with holes all work well. Decorate with ribbon.

Talk about

Talk about stories that include music: Bible stories such as Miriam dancing with tambourines after God's people crossed the Reed Sea (Exodus 15:9–21), and folk stories such as the musicians of Bremen or the little mermaid and her singing, or films such as *School of Rock*. What's your favourite song?

Musical instruments: hooters and didgeridoos

> **You will need:** Hollow card tubes (such as the insides of wrapping paper rolls), poster paints in different colours, cheap plastic kazoos, squeakers or hooters, lengths of ribbon, mediumweight card, sticky tape

Decorate hollow tubes with aboriginal spotty patterns (either dots of paint or small round stickers) to make didgeridoos. Have some cheap plastic kazoos, squeakers or hooters (can be found in supermarkets in party bag supplies sections) and decorate them with ribbons. You can add cardboard cones to them as megaphones to make them louder. Confiscate until worship time or all your leaders will hate you for ever.

Talk about

Talk about the power of sound to shatter glass at the right pitch, and how sound waves work by changing the pressure in the air. Have your ears ever been hurt by a sound?

Coloured sound

You will need: Pictures of musical instruments and other things that make sound, scissors, sheets of paper, PVA glue, paint sample leaflets

Have a supply of pictures of musical instruments and other things that make sound (children, grown-ups shouting or smiling, choirs, washing machines, pop groups, alarm clocks and so on) from shopping catalogues and magazines. Cut out the pictures and glue them to a sheet of paper. Then look through the colours in a paint sample leaflet and cut out the ones that match the noise 'colour' of all the noisy things you've chosen. Stick a coloured block next to each picture.

Talk about

Talk about what colour sounds might be if they had colours. Might trumpets be yellow? Could birdsong be green? Might someone telling you off be red?

Worship ribbons

You will need: Dowel or thin cardboard tubing, strips of crêpe paper, gift ribbon or cloth ribbon, sticky tape

Take a short piece of dowel or thin cardboard tubing and tape on strips of either crêpe paper, gift ribbon or cloth ribbon. Lightweight strips of scrap material can also be very effective. Judge the length of the strips by the size and coordination of the person making it. Any length between one and two metres works well. More professional ones can be made using anglers' swivels (see instructions under 'Using ribbons in church' on the Barnabas website) but probably don't make enough difference to justify the extra fiddling.

Talk about

Talk about the way we can worship God through movement as well as words.

CELEBRATION

Setting up the church or worship space

You will need: A supply of empty cardboard boxes, PowerPoint loaded with digital pictures of finished artwork (optional), samples of artwork from each activity station

Decorate the worship space with a wall of boxes ready set up at the front. If you are using PowerPoint, have this ready to display photos of artwork as everyone comes in. Comment on the artwork.

Song selection

Be bold, be strong (*Kidsource 1*, 17)
Life is like a big wide ocean (*Kidsource 1*, 232)
We are marching (*Kidsource 1*, 350)
As for me and my house (*Kidsource 1*, 12)
We are warriors (Doug Horley, *Humungous Song Book*, 90)

Talk

If you have manageable numbers, the people could be Joshua and his army marching around the church or worship space as you tell that part of the story.

Joshua was faced with a really big problem. Sometimes we too have to face really big problems.

Build up a wall of cardboard boxes.

Joshua's problem looked like this: it was a high wall, a strong wall round the city of Jericho. Somehow Joshua had to get into the city, but there was his big problem: the wall! He couldn't go round the back of it. He couldn't go over it. He couldn't go under it. He certainly couldn't go through it. Sometimes our problems feel a bit like that, too.

So Joshua prayed to God and God told him to do the strangest thing. He told Joshua to march silently round the wall six times. So that's what Joshua and his army did—round and round the wall six times in absolute silence. Then, on the seventh time, God told the priests to blow their trumpets. So I'll count to six and, on seven, can you all blow, shake or squeeze the instruments you've made to make a terrific noise?

Count to six, pause, and then say, 'Seven!'

And the problem came crashing down in front of them!

So when it looks as if there's no way through your problem, ask God for his help and he might just give you a really big surprise!

Prayer response

Lift your hands up as high as you can, as if you're in front of a really high wall.
Lord, sometimes our problems seem so massive that we can't imagine how to sort them.

Now bring your hands down to the floor with a rolling action, as if the wall is collapsing.
Help us to put our problems in your hands.

Lift your hands high again.
Let's all think of a really big problem, either a problem of our own or of someone else in the world.

Roll your hands down again.

Thank you, Lord, that you take all our problems into your own hands.

Final blessing

Lord, thank you that you have cared for your people throughout the world and throughout history. Help us to care for one another, loving each other through thick and thin. Amen

Messy Grace

May the grace of our Lord Jesus Christ (*Hold out your hands as if expecting a present*)
And the love of God (*Put your hands on your heart*)
And the fellowship of the Holy Spirit (*Hold hands*)
Be with us all now and for ever. Amen! (*Raise hands together on the word 'Amen'*)

Jesus' 'I am' sayings (and Christmas)

A series on Jesus' 'I am' sayings

UNIT 5

I am the true vine

AIM

To explore what a vine is like and what Jesus meant when he said these words, discovering truths about growth, fruitfulness and staying close to Jesus.

BIBLE BACKGROUND (John 15:1–11)

Jesus was talking about being the true vine in a conversation with his disciples very soon after the last supper and before Gethsemane, so he's using the image to encourage his friends to stick with him, even though the going is about to get really tough. Staying close to Jesus, loving him and trying to do what he wants will result in a vibrant, fruitful life. It will mean discipline and submitting to being 'pruned' from season to season, but this is God's way of making both us and his kingdom grow and be fruitful.

For children and adults who aren't familiar with the Bible and its imagery, there are considerations to take into account.

✢ Very few people in the UK have seen a vine or have any idea how to look after one. To Jesus and his friends, vines were as common and mundane as cabbages in Lincolnshire or apples in Hereford-shire. To us in the UK, vines are exotic and special, so the image becomes super-holy and distant.

✢ People won't have heard of the powerful image of the vineyard representing Israel or God's kingdom throughout the Bible, so much of the resonance of Jesus' words is lost.

✤ Many people in a literal-minded society will think 'I am a plant' is a really weird thing to say.

✤ The idea of discipline (or pruning) could easily be seen as a negative idea, suggesting a strict disciplinarian God rather than a Father-gardener who wants the best for his plants.

So our focus in this unit is on *fruitfulness, growth and togetherness*. By using fruit and vegetables common to our society, we try to regain some of the ordinary holiness of Jesus' image. But it's good to get to know what a vine is, as it's such a powerful image in Christianity and Judaism, so we include grapes and vines in among the apples and potatoes.

For some people, it's good to celebrate the simple idea that human life is about growth. Others may see that being a Christian is a great way to live, as the wholesome lovely side of being human will be encouraged to grow (love, joy, peace, patience and so on). This may be especially important for parents to see for their children as they grow up in a materialistic, greedy culture.

We also explore the idea that Jesus wants us to stay close to him through fellowship with other Christians and through talking to him personally. (Bible study may be one step too far for Messy Church people, but it's worth mentioning it.) The session links in well with Harvest festival, and you may want to use some of the artwork in the Harvest decorations for Sunday worship.

FOOD

Jacket potatoes with salad and fillings

Put out a bowl of salad and bowls containing baked beans, cheese, tuna and butter at regular intervals on the tables just before serving up the potatoes on plates. People can help themselves to salad and fillings.

Make it clear how many tables those bowls have to serve. It helps to ask one person to be in charge of their section of the tables and to organize the doling out of the fillings.

ACTIVITIES

Icing vines

You will need: Fondant icing coloured brown, green and purple, ivy-leaf biscuit cutter, paper plates

Roll brown icing into long thin branches. Roll out green icing and cut into leaf shapes using an ivy-leaf cutter. Roll purple icing into small balls and pile up as bunches of grapes. Build up a vine design on a small named paper plate. Ration each person with a set amount of icing or it will all vanish in the first five minutes.

Talk about
During this activity, talk about vines growing in vineyards. Perhaps people have seen some on holiday.

Frosted grapes

You will need: Bunch of grapes (washed), beaten egg white (or powdered egg white made up as per instructions on the pack), caster sugar, paper plates

Dip grapes one by one into beaten egg white and roll in caster sugar. Leave to dry on a paper plate.

Talk about
During this activity, talk about grapes growing on vines and being good to eat or to make into wine.

Apple bobbing

You will need: A baby bath, small apples (washed), towels and a mop

Fill the baby bath with water and float small apples in it. The apples have to be taken out of the water using only the teeth. Allow people to take the apple they catch away with them. Have a towel and mop handy.

Talk about

During this activity, talk about fruit and vegetables that grow in this country and whether they grow on trees or bushes or in the ground.

Interwoven vine branch bracelets

You will need: Balls of string or embroidery silks in different colours, masking tape, wooden beads

Make simple macramé bracelets from string by plaiting three different-coloured strands together. (Use the masking tape to secure the strands while you are braiding them.) Finish with a bead fastener.

Talk about

During this activity, talk about the way the string gets knotted together so that it's strong, about the way people are joined together in families, friendship groups and in church, and how God likes us to be close to him.

Grape treading

You will need: An old baby bath, cheap bath sponges, purple poster paint, lining wallpaper (unpasted), brown felt-tipped pens

Fill the bath full of sponges and purple poster paint. Tread in the bath with bare feet and walk down a very long piece of lining paper, which you have previously decorated with a very simple brown vine branch design. The footprints (especially the toes) look like bunches of grapes.

Put the end result down the centre of the worship space, or the nave, for the act of worship.

Talk about

During this activity, talk about traditional ways of pressing grapes for wine.

Hedgerow harvest plaque

You will need: Oasis foam, masking tape or coloured tape, small plastic saucers, a selection of leaves and berries

Using a plastic saucer and oasis foam fixed in place with tape, make up a small display using leaves and berries from local gardens.

Talk about

During this activity, talk about the lovely plants that grow in the wild and in gardens and how God makes them grow even if nobody sees them. He also gives berries and nuts for food for animals: he looks after his creation.

Potato printing

You will need: Waxy potatoes, sheets of paper, scraps of fabric or cheap hankies (from the market), poster paint, acrylic or fabric paint, old saucers, kitchen paper

Pre-cut some potatoes into geometric shapes, leaving some uncut for older children and adults to design their own prints. Pour a little paint into each saucer and print on paper or cloth.

Talk about
During this activity, talk about how useful potatoes are, where they grow and the sorts of ways people like to eat them—chips, mash and so on.

Vegetable modelling

You will need: A variety of vegetables, cocktail sticks, wobbly eyes and foam shapes

Turn vegetables into people and animals with the cocktail sticks, wobbly eyes and foam shapes.

Talk about
During this activity, talk about how vegetables are good for you, what wonderful shapes and colours they are and how God provides good things to eat.

Vine bookmarks

You will need: Rectangles of mediumweight card, sticky sequins, laminating machine (optional)

On a rectangle of card, draw a simple vine branch and the words 'Jesus said, "I am the true vine"'. Then stick on small sticky sequins in bunch shapes to make the bunches of grapes. You can laminate the result.

Talk about
During this activity, talk about how funny it was for Jesus to say 'I am the true vine' and wonder together what he might have meant. Did Jesus have green leaves coming out of his ears or grapes dangling from his fingers?

Collage

You will need: Sheet of mediumweight card, scraps of coloured paper, templates of leaves, grapes and letters, scraps of fabric, scissors, PVA glue, felt-tipped pens

Using templates of leaves, grapes and letters, cut out the shapes from paper and cloth scraps to make a collage for the noticeboard. Put the words 'Jesus said, "I am the true vine"' in the middle and make a border of vines round the outside.

Talk about
During this activity, talk about how things stick together best and what might be the glue that sticks people together.

CELEBRATION

Setting up the church or worship space

Decorate the worship space with the following items.

✤ If you can lay hands on some real vine trimmings, weave them in and out of the seats. (They wilt quickly so don't do this too far in advance.)

✤ Lay the grape-treading picture down the walkway into the worship space or church.

✤ Put a picture of a vine without grapes on a firm surface at the front.

You will also need:
PowerPoint loaded with digital pictures of finished artwork (optional), samples of artwork from each activity station, a dead branch, pencils, pieces of paper cut into the shape of a bunch of grapes (one per person), picture of tree with fruit

---

As everyone comes in, give them a 'bunch of grapes' shape to write on during the prayers. (You could cut out shapes from large stickers or Post-It notes so that they stick on as a display, or simply have paper shapes to place on a flat picture.) If you are using PowerPoint, have this ready to display photos of artwork as everyone comes in.

Song selection

I walk by faith (*Kidsource 1*, 177)
I belong to Jesus (*Kidsource 1*, 262)
I'm forever in your love (Doug Horley, *Humungous Song Book*, 39)
Father God, I wonder (*Kidsource 1*, 52)
Father, I place into your hands (*Kidsource 2*, 457)
Our God is a great big God (*Great Big God* CD, Vineyard)
God's love is so big (*Great Big God* CD, Vineyard)

Help me be your eyes, Lord Jesus (Doug Horley, *Humungous Song Book*, 25)
Jesus put this song into our hearts (with vineyard steps dance) (*Junior Praise 2*, 408)

Talk

Show a broken-off fruit tree branch and ask if it will ever grow apples again. Why not? Because it's dead—it isn't attached to the main tree any longer. Jesus said, 'I am the vine... remain in me and I will remain in you.' He wants us to stay close to him and to each other so that our lives aren't dead and empty like this branch, but have lots of fruit like this tree in the picture. We can stay close to Jesus by coming to church to be with other Christians or praying or reading the Bible.

Prayer response

Write or draw a prayer on a grape shape and come and place it on the prayer vine. It can be a please, thank you or sorry prayer.

Final blessing

Lord, thank you that you have made us to be together as part of your family throughout the world and throughout history. Help us to live as one family, loving each other through thick and thin. Amen

Messy Grace

May the grace of our Lord Jesus Christ (*Hold out your hands as if expecting a present*)
And the love of God (*Put your hands on your heart*)
And the fellowship of the Holy Spirit (*Hold hands*)
Be with us all now and for ever. Amen! (*Raise hands together on the word 'Amen'*)

UNIT 6

I am the light for the world

AIM

To explore the theme of light at a dark time of year, both actual light and the symbolism of light.

BIBLE BACKGROUND (John 8:12)

Jesus describes himself as the light for the world (John 8:12) and John picks up this theme throughout his Gospel from the very first chapter. The symbolism echoes through the Bible right from God's first recorded words, 'I command light to shine!' (Genesis 1:3); through the prophets, such as Isaiah writing, 'The people who walked in darkness have seen a great light' or, 'Arise, shine; for your light has come' (Isaiah 9:2; 60:1, NRSV); through the Gospels, where Jesus actually embodies light; on into the epistles, where Paul encourages the Philippians to 'shine like stars' (Philippians 2:15, NRSV); and features strongly in John's vision of a new heaven where no more lamps will be needed because God himself will be their light (Revelation 22:5). Light and dark are intriguing subjects to explore on both a physical and a symbolic level.

The session links in well with All Hallows or Non-Hallowe'en events. It would also go with Christmas or Candlemas or tie in with a Christingle service.

FOOD

Baguette pizza with garlic bread

Serve from the kitchen. Have salad in bowls on the tables.

ACTIVITIES

Light cards

You will need: Mediumweight card, coloured pencils

Make a card in either a candle shape or a lightbulb shape. Inside, write 'At this dark time of year, may the light of Jesus shine in you.'

Talk about
Talk about different sources of light and which are best for different purposes.

Stained-glass windows

You will need: Rectangles of dark card, tissue paper in different colours, PVA glue

Using rectangles of dark card in various sizes, pre-cut shapes of stars, crosses, moons, circles, fish and candles into them. Invite people to paste different-coloured tissue paper in ripped strips behind the card so that the strips stretch across the cut-out shapes. Encourage them to blend colours by pasting different-coloured strips close to each other. Display on a window.

Talk about
Talk about the way light transforms stained glass.

Lanterns

You will need: A4 coloured paper, scissors, sticky tape or PVA glue

Fold an A4 piece of coloured paper in half lengthways and make cuts over the fold line, approximately 1cm apart, without cutting up to the edge. Leave about 5cm margin on each side. Open out the paper, roll it round so that it makes a tall lantern shape with a kink in the middle and glue or tape the longer edges together to hold it in place. Add a paper handle over the top.

Talk about
Talk about festivals of light round the world. Light is a very powerful symbol for many different religions and peoples. What festivals of light do we know about? What might Jesus have meant when he said, 'I am the light for the world'?

Hats

You will need: Lightweight card, glitter, sequins, silver streamers, Christmas tree 'icicles' and shiny wrapping paper, stapler or sticky tape

Use the card, glitter and other materials to design and decorate a party hat. Stick together the component parts with staples or sticky tape.

Talk about
Talk about people you know who seem to have a light inside them: bright, cheery people or peaceful people.

Spiral decorations

You will need: Holographic card, strips of foil or shiny paper, PVA glue, cotton thread

Cut a spiral out of holographic card. Decorate it with thin strips of foil or shiny paper to dangle from it. Attach a thread to one end of the spiral and hang it in the light to twist and sparkle, 'catching the light'.

Talk about
Talk about sparkly things 'catching the light'. How can we 'catch the light' to make our lives sparkle?

Glittery stars

You will need: Mediumweight card, glitter, scissors, PVA glue, shiny ribbon, hole punch

Decorate cardboard stars with glitter. Punch a hole through the top of each star and hang up on shiny ribbon.

Talk about
Talk about light being on the move. Marvel at light waves travelling across the universe, so that we see a star here on earth years after the light actually sets out from that star.

Crystal jars

You will need: Jars with screw-on lids, clear glass beads (from craft shops), cotton thread, sticky tape

Thread a large 'crystal' bead on to a short piece of cotton. Tape the other end of the cotton to the inside lid of a jar and screw on the lid, so that the crystal dangles inside the jar.

Talk about
Talk about the way crystals reflect light from every surface. How might our lives reflect God's light in different ways?

Play dough

You will need: Play dough

Have fun with the play dough.

Talk about
Talk about what fun it is to make things and how, when we make things, we reflect God who is always making things.

Candle light

You will need: Large shallow bowl, water, selection of mirrors, floating candles, candle lighter or taper and box of matches

With adult supervision for your younger members, light floating candles using a taper and float them in a large glass bowl of water.

Older members may enjoy lighting them with a match. Place the bowl on a mirror, stand mirrors around it and enjoy the reflections. Have some small handbag mirrors for people to hold and experiment with. Wonder at the way the reflections go on into infinity. If you use scented candles, this is even more fun.

Talk about
Talk about reflections. How does a mirror reflect your face? How do you reflect God?

Candles to go

> **You will need**: Glass jars, glass paints, tealights, candle lighter or taper and box of matches

Decorate glass jars with glass paints and put a tealight inside.

Talk about
Talk about the way we can take Jesus' light with us wherever we go, even into the darkest places.

CELEBRATION

Setting up the church or worship space

> **You will need**: Different sorts of lights (see below), PowerPoint loaded with digital pictures of finished artwork (optional), samples of artwork from each activity station

Decorate the worship space with a display of different sorts of lights: lamps, candles, pictures of car headlights, camera flash, lighthouse, torches and so on. If you are using PowerPoint, have this ready to display photos of artwork as everyone comes in. Comment on the artwork.

Song selection

Light of the world (*Songs of Fellowship 3*, 1419)
Jesus is greater than the greatest hero (*Kidsource 1*, 296)
We are bright lights (*Kidsource 1*, 362)
Colours of day (*Kidsource 2*, 433)
Jesus be the centre (*Songs of Fellowship 3*, 1377)

Talk

Have you ever been in the dark? What does it feel like? Scary? Fun? Peaceful? Dangerous?

Imagine a city in the dark, all blacked out. The whole city would be in darkness. Without any source of light, what would it be like trying to walk along the pavement? Or driving your car with no lights? Or finding your way home? Or finding the people you're looking for?

When Jesus was at a special festival in Jerusalem, it was night time. Because there were no street lamps in those days, it was very dark—except that, during this festival, they lit four great lamps in the temple, which lit up the city. Suddenly everyone could see almost as much as in the daytime! They didn't bump into things, they could see where they were going and they could find whoever they were looking for. Jesus saw the light of the lamps coming from the temple. He saw what a huge difference the light made to the city and he shouted out, 'I'm the light for the world!' Not just for the people in the city of Jerusalem, but for everyone in the world.

I wonder, when you look at these lights here, which you think is most like Jesus? Is it the candle with its gentle flame? Or the camera flash that shows up all the details in a photo? Or car headlights that let you see where you're going? Or a lighthouse that stops you crashing into a rock?

Now let's turn those thoughts into prayers.

Prayer response

Ask some people to come and choose one of the lights. As each different light becomes the focus, start off: 'Lord Jesus, thank you that you are like a... (torch) because...' Ask someone to finish the sentence off, or use some of the ideas from the talk earlier. All say 'Amen' at the end of each idea.

Final blessing

Lord, thank you that your light shines in your people throughout the world and throughout history. Help us to shine, loving each other through thick and thin. Amen

Messy Grace

May the grace of our Lord Jesus Christ (*Hold out your hands as if expecting a present*)
And the love of God (*Put your hands on your heart*)
And the fellowship of the Holy Spirit (*Hold hands*)
Be with us all now and for ever. Amen! (*Raise hands together on the word 'Amen'*)

UNIT 7

I am the good shepherd

AIM

To understand the way Jesus guides us and leads us in the same way that a shepherd looks after his sheep.

BIBLE BACKGROUND (John 10:7–11)

There are two 'I am' sayings tied closely together in this passage, as Jesus also says, 'I am the gate for the sheep' in verse 7. Even if people have never seen a sheep or met a shepherd, the image of someone who is closely linked to those he cares for, yet is different from them, who defends and protects them and provides for them, is powerful and readily understandable. Ezekiel also writes a great deal about the bad leaders of Israel being like bad shepherds, and God having to step in to be the good shepherd (Ezekiel 34), which gives an interesting dimension to Jesus' words.

FOOD

Shepherd's pie, cottage pie or gardener's pie

This is an all-in-one dish to be served from the kitchen. Have the gardener's pie ready for those who want the veggie alternative.

ACTIVITIES

Sheep collage

You will need: Sheets of sugar paper, painting materials, cotton wool, brushes, PVA glue, jars of clean water

Add cotton wool sheep on to a backdrop of fields, hills and water. Someone artistic might want to add a shepherd tackling a hungry wolf.

Talk about
Talk about where sheep like to live.

Spinning wool

You will need: Someone who can give a demonstration of spinning or carding wool for everyone to watch.

Talk about
Talk about where wool comes from.

Cotton wool sheep badges

You will need: Pre-cut head shapes from black paper, googly eyes, cotton wool pads, PVA glue, safety pins, sticky tape

Glue some googly eyes (available from craft shops or larger supermarkets) on to your pre-cut head shapes. Glue the head on to a circular cotton wool pad. Tape a safety pin to the back and wear as a badge.

Talk about

Talk about the way sheep copy each other and don't think for themselves. (God doesn't want us to be mindless sheep, but to get to know him for ourselves.)

Sheep biscuits

You will need: Rich Tea biscuits, white glacé icing, sweet strings, Smarties

Decorate a Rich Tea biscuit with a blob of white icing for the sheep, sweet strings for legs and a Smartie head. To tell the truth, it doesn't look much like a sheep to an impartial observer, but it tastes very nice.

Talk about

Talk about the way a shepherd finds food for his sheep to eat.

Sheep pen construction

You will need: Junk art items, masking or sticky tape

Have a large pile of junk and lots of tape. Make a sheep pen out of the junk.

Talk about

Talk about the way a sheep pen keeps the sheep safe from things outside and how a good shepherd sleeps across the opening so that the wolves have to face him before they can get to the sheep.

Name placards

> **You will need:** Sheets of A4 paper, coloured sticker shapes, glitter, paints and colouring materials

Draw your name in large hollow letters. Fill in the letters with stickers, glitter, paints and colouring.

Talk about
Talk about the way the shepherd knows each of his sheep by name.

Rolling marbles

> **You will need:** Marbles, poster paints, lining wallpaper (unpasted)

Roll marbles in paint and then roll them across large sheets of paper as if they are wandering sheep leaving a trail behind them.

Talk about
Talk about the way sheep nibble their way thoughtlessly away from the shepherd and end up being far away from him without intending to leave him.

Model sheep

> **You will need:** Cardboard tubes, cotton wool, mediumweight card, drinking straws, PVA glue

Make a sheep out of a cardboard tube, lots of cotton wool and a big cheerful face drawn on to a circle of paper or card and glued to one end of the tube. Legs made from straws or folded stiff card can be added.

Talk about
Talk about what sheep give us.

Pompoms

You will need: Mediumweight card, balls of wool, scissors

Make small pompoms. Place two doughnut-shaped pieces of card together and wind wool round and round them until it's impossible to fit any more wool through the hole in the centre. Cut through all the layers of wool on the outer edge of the circle. Tie a piece of wool around the centre of the pompom, in between the pieces of card. Secure tightly. Cut off the card.

Talk about
Talk about all the things we use wool for.

Pocket psalm

You will need: Empty matchboxes, sheets of A4 paper in white, blue and dark brown, mediumweight card in white, black and brown, green colouring crayons, spent matches, scissors, PVA glue, Psalm 23 printed on tiny pieces of paper

Cover a matchbox with white paper. On the top, glue a piece of blue paper. On the underneath, glue a dark piece of paper. Colour the tray in green. Make one or more tiny sheep out of white or black card folded in half so that the sheep stands upright. Make a tiny shepherd's crook out of brown card. Have four spent matchsticks to make up the sheep pen.

Use these 'props' to tell a story about the shepherd taking the sheep from the pen to green fields of grass (the tray) and to still waters (the blue) and, even in the valley of the shadow of death (the dark shape), how the shepherd sees the sheep safely through to the other side. For older people, have versions of Psalm 23 printed on to a tiny piece of paper that they can fit into the matchbox with the sheep, pen and crook.

Talk about
Talk about the way a shepherd cares for the sheep and goes everywhere with them. David was a shepherd before he became a king and he wrote this famous psalm about a shepherd.

CELEBRATION

Setting up the church or worship space

You will need: A shepherd's crook, PowerPoint loaded with digital pictures of finished artwork (optional), samples of artwork from each activity station

Create a sheepfold at the front of the worship space out of a square of chairs. If you are using PowerPoint, have it ready to display photos of artwork as everyone comes in. Comment on the artwork.

Song selection

I am special (*Kidsource 1*, 62)
My Jesus, my Saviour (*Songs of Fellowship 2*, 935)
Every move I make (Integrity Music, *Shout to the Lord Kids 1* CD and music book)

King of love (Doug Horley, *Humungous Song Book*, 50)
Wonderful Lord (Doug Horley, *Humungous Song Book*, 98)
Will you come and follow me? (*Songs of Fellowship 2*, 1102)
I, the Lord of sea and sky (*Songs of Fellowship 2*, 830)

Talk

Ask: Have you all had a good time? What have you been making? Lots of things to do with sheep…

I've brought along a shepherd's crook. Sometimes bishops carry a crook. Why do you think they do that?

Jesus said 'I am the good shepherd.' We're all his sheep. Say 'baa!' Jesus looks after us just as a good shepherd looks after his sheep.

Jesus knows the name of every one of his sheep.

Call out names of people. They answer 'baa!' and come to the front.

Jesus makes sure his sheep have what we need. He leads us to the place where there's the best grass to eat.

Lead the flock to one side of the church.

He leads us to the place where there's refreshing water to drink.

Lead them to the other side.

Jesus keeps his sheep safe. At night he leads us into the sheepfold, so that we are kept safe from danger—especially from the wolf.

Lead them into the sheepfold made of chairs or from the craft earlier.

Jesus says, 'I'm the gate for the sheep.' He lies down across the entrance to keep us safe from the wolf.

Lie down in the entrance to the sheepfold.

When the wolf attacks, Jesus doesn't run away. He faces the danger, and protects us.

Stand up with the crook, ready to protect the flock.

We know that Jesus really cares because he was ready to die for us on the cross. He gave up his life for his flock. Jesus is our good shepherd; it's great to be his sheep. Let's hear it again: *Baa!!!*

Prayer response

Leader: For being our good shepherd…
All: Thank you, Jesus.
Leader: For leading us to good places…
All: Thank you, Jesus.
Leader: For keeping us safe…
All: Thank you, Jesus.
Leader: For protecting us from evil…
All: Thank you, Jesus.
Leader: For dying for us…
All: Thank you, Jesus.

Final blessing

Lord, thank you that you love and protect your people throughout the world and throughout history. Help us to care for each other too, loving each other through thick and thin. Amen

Messy Grace

May the grace of our Lord Jesus Christ (*Hold out your hands as if expecting a present*)
And the love of God (*Put your hands on your heart*)
And the fellowship of the Holy Spirit (*Hold hands*)
Be with us all now and for ever. Amen! (*Raise hands together on the word 'Amen'*)

Messy Christmas

AIM

To enjoy the messiness of Christmas time.

BIBLE BACKGROUND (Luke 2:1–21; Matthew 1:18—2:15)

Jesus' birth was a very messy time, so it's appropriate to celebrate it in the context of Messy Church. It's easy to forget about the smells and dirt of that first Christmas. Easy, too, to forget that what is nicely packaged as a tidy story for us actually spreads over several years and several countries, from Gabriel's announcement to the flight to Egypt. It draws in messy people—the shepherds most notably, but also the travelling wise men from a far-off country. It shows us how God works with people on the edge, such as the teenager Mary from the back of beyond. In fact, Mary's song (Luke 1:46–55) tells beautifully of how God turns away from the rich and powerful and works through the humble, messy people on the edge of society.

FOOD

Chicken casserole

Serve from the kitchen. Have bread on the tables.

ACTIVITIES

Print wrapping paper

You will need: Large sheets of paper, Christmas-shaped blocks, foam shapes or stamps, coloured inks or poster paints

Using Christmas-shaped blocks, foam shapes or stamps, print large sheets of paper that can be used as wrapping paper.

Talk about
Talk about the visit of the wise men and the gifts they brought Jesus.

Ice cream cone angel

You will need: Ice cream cones, fondant icing in white, yellow and brown, silver balls, gold paper doilies or thin card, paper plates, piping set (optional)

Make an angel out of an ice cream cone with fondant icing over it for a robe, an icing head with silver balls for eyes, yellow or brown icing for hair and a gold doily or card cut up for wings. Stand the angel on a plate and, if desired, pipe frilly icing round the base of the cone for decoration.

Talk about
Talk about the part God's messengers played in the birth of Jesus—Gabriel announcing the news to Mary and to the shepherds, and the choir of angels.

Donkey dung

You will need: Fondant icing, cocoa powder, paper plates

Mix cocoa powder with fondant icing. Form into small and revolting pats. Place on named paper plates.

Talk about

Talk about the messy journey and the messy stable. (Mary may have travelled on a donkey, as it was about 80 miles from Nazareth to Bethlehem.)

Gift box

You will need: Mediumweight card, Christmas stickers, wrapped chocolate sweets, scissors, ruler, PVA glue, pencils or felt-tipped pens

Make a gift box and decorate it with Christmas stickers. Put a wrapped chocolate inside it and write a label for a friend or family member.

Talk about

Talk about the gifts that we give others and the gifts God has given us.

Hanging decorations

You will need: Gold and silver card, glitter, PVA glue, hole punch, shiny gift ribbon

Make snowflakes out of gold and silver card. Cover with glitter. Punch a hole and thread through a piece of shiny gift ribbon.

Talk about

Talk about celebrations in the Christian year and how we make Jesus' birth a special occasion by decorating our houses and Christmas trees to look festive and cheerful.

Candles in holders

You will need: Small pieces of oasis, plastic flowerpot saucers, birthday cake candles, holly leaves, berries and ivy

Stick small pieces of oasis into plastic flowerpot saucers. Stick a birthday cake candle in the oasis and decorate with holly leaves, berries and ivy.

Talk about

Talk about Jesus coming as the light for the world, to make dark places bright.

Christmas cards

You will need: Mediumweight card, collage materials, coloured pencils or felt-tipped pens, glitter, PVA glue, ruler, scissors

Make a Christmas card to send to a family member, perhaps in the church family. There are dozens of Christmas card designs in books and on the Internet.

Talk about

Talk about the way Christmas is a good time to remember how special friends and families are, because Jesus didn't just appear by magic—he was born into a family.

Christmas card cut-outs

You will need: Old Christmas cards, lining wallpaper (unpasted), scissors, PVA glue

Have a large heap of last year's Christmas cards. Ask the children to sort through them and cut out pictures from any that are to do with the biblical Christmas story. Glue the pictures on to a large wall display in groupings: the angel and Mary, the journey to Bethlehem, the place Jesus was born, the shepherds, wise men, star and so on.

Talk about

Talk about the Christmas story and how lots of extra bits have been added that aren't actually in the Bible—robins and snowmen and holly and so on.

Straw and hay

You will need: Sheets of paper, PVA glue, clean straw, hay and twigs, large porridge oats

Draw a simple outline picture of a nativity scene. Fill the different areas with glue and cover them with straw, hay, twigs and oats, to show the sorts of bits and pieces that might have been around when Jesus was born.

Talk about

Talk about the clean hospitals where babies are born today and the messiness of the place where Jesus was born.

Hard work babies

You will need: Real babies or toy dolls, baby equipment (feeding bottles, nappies, baby bath and so on), baby clothes and toys

Ask some parents to bring in their babies and show everyone how to cuddle a baby, put on a nappy, feed a baby, bath it, play with it and so on. Alternatively, ask children to bring in their dolls and show everyone how to look after a baby, using the dolls as a model.

Talk about
Talk about what it's like to bring up babies and all the messiness of it.

CELEBRATION

Setting up the church or worship space

You will need: PowerPoint loaded with digital pictures of finished artwork (optional), samples of artwork from each activity station, dustbins and full bin bags, a manger

Decorate the worship space with some smelly dustbins and full bin bags. Arrange a manger in front of them. If you are using PowerPoint, have it ready to display photos of artwork as everyone comes in. Comment on the artwork.

Song selection

Traditional carols of your choice.

Talk

I wish you all a Messy Christmas! That's not right—it should be 'Merry'.

When we think about it, though, the first Christmas was really quite messy. There was no room for Jesus in the inn, so he had to be laid in an animal's feeding trough, probably still containing bits of half-chewed food and mucky straw. The stable was probably dirty and smelly. After all, animals will be animals...

And what about the shepherds? They weren't scrubbed clean and cute like those we see on Christmas cards. Real shepherds were grubby, greasy, smelly (they had nowhere to wash their socks) and reeking of stinky wet sheep. But they were the first people to be told about Jesus' birth and to be invited to visit the Saviour of the world.

Christmas is messy because that's what God intended. Jesus is God's Mess-iah. He's come to be with us in our messy world, to help us sort out the mess and to have a fresh start.

Mary and Joseph and the shepherds were ordinary people just like you and me. They remind us that Jesus was born for messy people just like you and me. And the sheep remind us that Jesus is God's Messiah for the whole of our messy world.

Prayer response

Leader   Think of something you'd like to thank God for.

Pause.

Leader   We're all going to shout our thanks together: Thank you, Father, for...

All shout it out together.

Leader: Now think of someone who needs God's help.

Pause.

Leader: We're going to whisper this prayer together: Please, Father, help…

All whisper it together.

Leader: We ask these prayers in Jesus' name.

All AMEN!

Final blessing

Lord, thank you for the gift of your Son, Jesus. Help us to care for each other this Christmas and to show your love to those we meet. Amen

Messy Grace

May the grace of our Lord Jesus Christ *(Hold out your hands as if expecting a present)*
And the love of God *(Put your hands on your heart)*
And the fellowship of the Holy Spirit *(Hold hands)*
Be with us all now and for ever. Amen! *(Raise hands together on the word 'Amen')*

New life
(including Easter
and Pentecost)

A series on new life

UNIT 9

Creation

AIM

To see that God is a messy creator God.

BIBLE BACKGROUND (Genesis 1:1—2:4)

The beautiful creation story in Genesis reminds us of God as the origin of everything, including our own creativity. It is a key story to explore and wonder at, as it shows God as the creator of the world we live in and one who is intimately involved in that world. The story gives us a sense of identity and purpose as his people, put here to look after the earth. It is a story that can be enjoyed on many different levels. It is also important to give everyone an opportunity to wonder at the created world around them and to open their eyes to the miracle of life.

FOOD

Hot sausage rolls and salad

Serve the sausage rolls from the kitchen and have bowls of salad on the tables for people to help themselves. Have some vegetarian rolls available, too.

ACTIVITIES

Primordial slime

You will need: Cornflour, water, mixing bowl, kitchen paper

Mix up cornflour and water to make a sloppy goo. Look—it's liquid but when you squeeze it in your hand, it goes solid!

Talk about
Talk about the way there was no life on earth until God made things live. Perhaps there was just gloopy mud all over the planet.

Creation scene

You will need: Art materials, lining wallpaper (unpasted)

Draw, colour and cut out your favourite part of the creation story on paper and stick it on to the right setting on a large backdrop, with just land, sea and sky already sketched in.

Talk about
Talk about the different things God made on each day.

Junk animals

You will need: Art materials, junk craft materials

Use the junk to make a weird and wonderful tree, animal, fish or bird.

Talk about
Talk about the way God made everything out of nothing.

Thank you cards

> **You will need:** Pictures of the world downloaded from the
> Internet or from magazines, mediumweight card, art
> materials, PVA glue, scissors

Use pictures of the world downloaded from the Internet or from
magazines to decorate a card and send it to someone who you'd like
to remind about the beauty of the world and the loving care of God.

Talk about
Talk about different ways to say 'thank you' to God for the world he's
made for us.

Day three kebabs

> **You will need:** A selection of fresh fruits (see below),
> wooden kebab sticks

Have small pieces of fruit cut up: grapes, berries, apple (sprinkled
with lemon juice), orange, melon, pineapple, kiwi, banana (in lemon
juice). Select a variety of fruit pieces and make up a tasty kebab on a
wooden kebab stick.

Talk about
Talk about the variety of plant life and how essential trees and plants
are to the balance of the world.

Edible Eden

You will need: Sheet of heavyweight card, greaseproof paper, tin foil, cocktail sticks, grapefruits, grapes, pick 'n' mix sweets (see below)

Make an edible landscape. On a huge sheet of sturdy card covered with clean greaseproof paper, make hills out of halved grapefruits covered in foil. Into these, stick 'trees' made from green sweets and grapes on cocktail sticks. Make rivers from blue stringy sweets. Have a desert made out of sherbert or flavoured sugar. Chocolate animals and jelly bears can roam the woodlands. Fizzy fish can swim in the rivers. Best to go and raid the pick 'n' mix and see what inspires you.

Talk about
Talk about the way the world was perfect in the beginning. Here you're making a very yummy world, but even this is nowhere near as wonderful as the first garden of Eden was.

Paper people

You will need: Lining wallpaper (unpasted), drawing equipment, scissors, books on different world cultures

Take a long strip of paper and fold it concertina-wise. Draw a human figure on the top piece, making sure the hands and feet touch the edges—don't cut through these but cut out the rest of the outline through the thicknesses of the paper. Open out the chain of people holding hands and draw different faces and clothes on to each figure. You might like to put each of them in clothes of different countries and colour the faces different colours. Have some reference books to hand to inspire you.

Talk about
Talk about the way God made us 'fearfully and wonderfully', with so many brilliant design features.

Pipe cleaner bugs

You will need: Pipe cleaners (from craft shops), googly eyes, PVA glue, *Guinness Book of Records* (optional)

Design your own bug from pipe cleaners. Remember, insects have six legs, a head, thorax and abdomen. Add googly eyes with glue.

Talk about
Talk about the wide range of sizes of creatures—the biggest and the smallest. Use the *Guinness Book of Records* for some examples.

Cocktail bar

You will need: A selection of fruit juices (see below), lemonade, drinking straws, cocktail umbrellas, ice cubes, paper cups

Have a variety of fruit juices (try to include kiwi juice as its bright green colour is peculiarly horrible when mixed with other juices). Mix up some weird and wonderful cocktails using the ingredients and decorations.

Talk about
Talk about vitamins in fruits and healthy, balanced diets.

Earth balloons

You will need: Blue balloons, black marker pens, luggage labels, balloon pump (optional)

On uninflated blue balloons, draw the outlines of continents in black marker pen. Blow up the balloons and tie luggage labels on to them, saying 'Fragile Handle With Care'.

Talk about

Talk about the fragile nature of the earth and how we should look after it.

CELEBRATION

Setting up the church or worship space

You will need: A selection of globes, natural objects (see below), PowerPoint loaded with digital pictures of finished artwork (optional), samples of artwork from each activity station

Have all the globes you can find on display in the worship space. Have a selection of interesting natural objects for the prayers, such as feathers, apples, small branches, stones, fossils, jugs of water, leaves and shells and so on. If you are using PowerPoint, have this ready to display photos of artwork as everyone comes in.

Say, 'We've been having a very creative time. Look at the things we've made! We enjoy being creative, making things. That's not surprising because we were made by a very creative God who loves making things.'

Song selection

Lovely jubbly (Doug Horley, *Humungous Song Book*, 58)
Have we made our God too small? (*Kidsource 1*, 96)
Our God is a great big God (*Great Big God*, Vineyard CD)
Great great brill brill (Doug Horley, *Humungous Song Book*, 66)

Talk

The Bible isn't just one book, it's a whole library of books. The first is called Genesis, which means 'beginnings'. It starts with the words, 'In the beginning God created the heavens and the earth.'

It tells the story of the beginning of the universe. It tells it in a special storytelling way, so that we can remember it and learn from it.

In the beginning there was absolutely nothing... except God—nothing else until God created the universe, the heavens and the earth.

Then God said, 'I command light to shine.' And light started shining.

He separated the light from the darkness.

He called the light 'Day' and the darkness he called 'Night'.

God saw the light and he said, 'It's good.' And that was the first day.

Then God said, 'Let there be a great blue dome above the earth.'

He separated the water on the earth from the water above the earth, and he called the great blue dome 'Sky'.

God saw the sky he'd made and said, 'It's good.' And that was the second day.

Then God commanded the dry ground to appear. He called the dry ground 'Land' and the water he called 'Sea'.

God said, 'Let the earth produce all kinds of plants with seeds and all kinds of trees that bear fruit.' And the land was covered with grasses and plants, flowers and trees of every kind.

God saw it all and said, 'It's good.' And that was the third day.

Then God said, 'Let there be two lights in the sky: the sun to shine by day and the moon to shine by night, to mark the days, weeks, months and years.' Oh, and he also made the stars.

God saw them all and said, 'It's good.' And that was the fourth day.

Then God said, 'Let the waters teem with living creatures—all kinds of fish and eels and crabs and whales, and let the skies be filled with flying birds...'

God saw them all and said, 'It's good.' And that was the fifth day.

Then God commanded the earth to be full of living creatures of all kinds of shapes and sizes—from tiny bugs to huge dinosaurs, animals that crawl, climb, walk, wriggle, grunt, squawk, whistle, roar and buzz.

Then God said, 'Now let's make people. I want them to be like me, and they can look after all the living things in my world.'

So God created people, men and women. He blessed us and gave us this earth to live on and to look after.

God looked at all he'd made and said, 'It's very good.' And that was the sixth day.

God's wonderful creation was complete. So on the seventh day he rested.

On the seventh day it was time to enjoy everything that God had made.

And that's the Bible story of the beginning of the universe.

In groups, families or all together, ask some or all of these questions.

* Which part of this story is your favourite part?
* Which part is the most mysterious?
* How do you think God feels about the part of the world you live in?
* How can you help to look after God's world?

Prayer response

Give out the natural objects, one per mixed group of adults and children, and ask the groups to pass their object round the group. As each person takes it, they say 'thank you' to God for something about the object—for example, its beauty, age, detail or usefulness, or that it reminds them of someone or something.

Final blessing

Lord, thank you for the gift of your world. Help us to live as one family, and care for everything you have made. Amen

Messy Grace

May the grace of our Lord Jesus Christ *(Hold out your hands as if expecting a present)*
And the love of God *(Put your hands on your heart)*
And the fellowship of the Holy Spirit *(Hold hands)*
Be with us all now and for ever. Amen! *(Raise hands together on the word 'Amen')*

UNIT 10

A new start

AIM

To see how God gave the world a chance for a new start.

BIBLE BACKGROUND (Genesis 6:1—9:17)

We keep the focus on God's love for the world and his re-creation of it after the story about Noah and the flood, rather than the reasons for the flood itself. This fits in well with the theme of the series (new life) and the overall emphasis of the Bible story, that of a God who always gives another chance, who always holds out hope in the most desperate of situations. In our own lives, the story encourages us never to despair but always to look out for the way through the situation to a resurrection truth.

FOOD

Fish fingers and potato wedges with peas

Serve fish fingers and wedges from the kitchen to avoid fighting over the wedges, and have peas on the tables.

ACTIVITIES

Rainbow bottles

You will need: Beads in the colours of the rainbow or 'sands' in the seven colours of the rainbow, made from salt mixed with a teaspoon of powder poster paint (rainbow colours) per 1kg bag of salt, clear plastic bottles

Use the coloured beads or coloured 'sands' to fill clear plastic bottles with layers of rainbow colours, starting with violet and finishing with red (violet, indigo, blue, green, yellow, orange and red). Seal them tightly!

Talk about
Talk about the rainbow being a sign of God's promise that he would never flood the whole earth again.

Animal masks

You will need: Pre-cut animal mask shapes, colouring pencils or felt-tipped pens, thin card tubes or small garden canes, masking tape

Pre-cut mask shapes for everyone to decorate. Tape the finished mask on to a short piece of tube or a thin garden cane, so that the mask can be held in front of the face.

Talk about
During this activity, talk about the wonderful variety of animals in our world and how much God loves them.

Valentine animal cards

You will need: Pictures of animal pairs (old greetings cards or the Internet are a good source for these), mediumweight card, scissors, drawing materials, PVA glue

Use the pictures to make loving animals cards, or create your own designs using the pictures as templates. If appropriate, this might be a good Valentine's Day card.

Talk about
Talk about pets and how much we love them.

Giant ark puzzle

You will need: Large sheets of mediumweight card, colouring pencils or felt-tipped pens, scissors, references for Noah's ark from books or the Internet

Draw a simple picture of Noah's ark on a large sheet of card and cut it into16 pieces. Each person takes one of the pieces and colours it in. When each piece is coloured, everyone can then make the jigsaw up into its complete picture. Duplicate the activity so that everyone can take part.

Talk about
Talk about the way the ark kept Noah and his family safe through the dreadful flood.

Edible arks

You will need: Cocktail sausages, cooked and cooled, cheese slices, cucumber, cocktail sticks, paper plates

Make a boat on a paper plate. The boat's body is a cold cocktail sausage with a cocktail stick mast supporting a cheese slice sail. A pennant of a cucumber slice triangle flies from the top of the mast. (Use vegetarian sausages as an alternative option.)

Talk about
During this activity, talk about what food might have been eaten on the ark.

Origami boats

You will need: Sheets of A4 paper, scissors, pens, cola bottle sweets, an old baby bath

Make a boat out of folded paper (see page 205 for instructions) and give it a name, written on the side. A 'cola bottle' sweet could be given with which to launch it into a baby bath.

Talk about
During this activity, talk about how small the ark was compared with the great flood.

Doves

> **You will need**: Mediumweight card, scissors, sheets of A4 paper, white feathers, PVA glue

Make a dove from a card template (see page 206 for instructions) with a slit cut through its tummy and a piece of paper folded into a concertina for wings. Decorate with feathers.

Talk about
Talk about the dove's role in the story and the way it has come to be a symbol of peace.

Woodwork

> **You will need**: Ready-made boat shapes cut from balsa wood, scraps of balsa wood, hammer, nails

Have some ready-made boat shapes in wood, about 2cm thick and 10cm long by 6cm wide. Under supervision, nail on a 4cm square block of wood, 2cm thick, to make an upper deck to the ark.

Talk about
Talk about the way Noah had to be a carpenter to make the ark and how Joseph and Jesus were carpenters, too.

Rainsticks

> **You will need**: Strong cardboard tubes, polystyrene packaging, beads, dried peas or rice, masking tape, colouring pencils or paint and brushes

Loosely fill a cardboard tube with pieces of polystyrene packaging (the sort that looks like Cheesy Wotsits). Spoon in two tablespoons of beads, dried peas or rice. Seal firmly and decorate the outside. When the rainstick is tipped, the peas will slowly make their way through the polystyrene packaging, making a sound like that of gentle rain.

Talk about
Talk about what the rain must have sounded like from inside the ark.

Aquaplay

> **You will need:** Old baby bath, water, water toys

Play with water toys together.

Talk about
Talk about how wonderful water is when it's in the right place and how dangerous it can be when there's too much of it or when it's in the wrong place.

CELEBRATION

Setting up the church or worship space

> **You will need:** PowerPoint loaded with digital pictures of finished artwork (optional), samples of artwork from each activity station

Bring the large jigsaw pictures of the ark into the worship area. Have some cuddly animals in some of the seats. If you are using PowerPoint, have it ready to display photos of artwork as everyone comes in.

Song selection

Rise and shine (*Kidsource 1*, 288)
Faith as small as a mustard seed (Doug Horley, *Humungous Song Book*, 15)

Talk

Tell the story of Noah, with sound effects and actions from everyone as indicated below.

Long, long ago, the world was in a bit of a mess. People had forgotten about God. And when people forget about God, they forget about being good to each other. They were doing terrible things. They were LYING (*mutter to your neighbour*) and STEALING (*pickpocket your neighbour*) and MURDERING (*pretend to strangle an imaginary person in front of you*).

God was very sad that the world was in such a mess and he decided he had to clean it up, but he loved the earth so much that he didn't want to destroy it completely. So he looked around for just one person who loved God and could help him save the earth. And God saw Noah.

God spoke to Noah and he said, 'Noah, I'm going to send an enormous flood to clean up the earth. You must build a big boat in the desert. When the boat is built, you must take your family and two of every sort of animal, bird and creepy-crawly on board.'

It was a rather strange thing, to build a boat in the middle of the desert, but Noah always did what God liked, so he and his family started to build a big boat. (*Cut trees down*) CHOP, CHOP. (*Saw the wood*) OOH-AH, OOH-AH. (*Hammer nails*) BANG, OUCH, BANG, OUCH!

And when the big boat was finished, Noah brought on board two of every kind of animal, every kind of bird and every kind of creepy crawly. The LITTLE SQUEAKY ONES (*ee, ee, ee*), the FAT AND FUNNY ONES (*monkey noises and pig grunts*) and the BIG SCARY ONES (*roar*). And God shut the door (*bang*).

Now, to clean things up, you need a lot of water. So God sent the RAIN (*clap hands slowly, then faster and more loudly*). Then he brought the underground water bubbling up and bursting all over the land. He gathered up all the clouds from round the earth and exploded them like water bombs. He pulled all the rivers and seas together and sent them charging over the dry land. He shovelled up the snow from the mountaintops and threw it down from the sky. He sent blizzards and monsoons and hurricanes and tidal waves—God sent the flood.

The boat was tossed on the waves for nearly a year—and what a year that was (*hold stomach and sway*). Then God sent the wind and the sun to dry out the earth like clothes on a washing line.

The boat came to rest on a high mountain called Ararat. When God had dried up the flood, Noah opened the door and out came the animals—the BIG SCARY ONES, the FAT AND FUNNY ONES and the LITTLE SQUEAKY ONES. Then, out came Noah's family, and there in the sky above them they saw a miracle! Wrapped round the earth, like a ribbon round a present, was a huge RAINBOW.

And God said, 'The rainbow is a sign of my promise to you that I will never again flood the whole earth. As long as the earth stands, there will be springtime and harvest, heat and cold, summer and winter, day and night.'

So when we see a rainbow, we can think of the way God gave the earth a new start through one single person who loved God. And next time we meet, at the Easter Messy Church, we will be thinking of another time God gave us a new start through one single person who loved God.

Prayer response

Say: Let's stand in the colours of the rainbow. If you're wearing red, orange or pink, stand over here; yellow and green over here; and blues or purples over here.

Red group: red is the colour of danger. Think of someone or somewhere in danger that needs God's love.

Green and yellow group: these are the colours for new growth. Think of a country that needs God's love to grow in it.

Blue: that can be a sad colour, so think of someone or somewhere sad that needs God's love. If you can't think of anyone for your colour, think of someone you know who is sad.

Lord, we pray for everyone in danger. Please help… (*Everyone shouts out the names together*).

Lord, we pray for everyone who needs your love to grow in them. Please let your love grow in… (*Everyone shouts out the names together*).

Lord, we pray for everyone who is sad. Please be close to… (*Everyone shouts out the names together*).

Rainbow God, thank you for all the new starts you give us.

Final blessng

Lord, thank you that we are one big family of your people throughout the world and throughout history. Help us to live as one family, loving each other as you love us. Amen

Messy Grace

May the grace of our Lord Jesus Christ (*Hold out your hands as if expecting a present*)

And the love of God (*Put your hands on your heart*)

And the fellowship of the Holy Spirit (*Hold hands*)

Be with us all now and for ever. Amen! (*Raise hands together on the word 'Amen'*)

UNIT 11

New life in Jesus (Easter)

AIM

To see the way God gives us a chance for new life through Jesus' death and resurrection.

BIBLE BACKGROUND
(Luke 22:1–20, 29–54; 23:1–25, 44–56; 24:1–12)

This may be the only Easter service many of the members will attend, so you need to squeeze the whole Maundy Thursday / Good Friday / Easter Sunday narrative into one short service. The Easter narrative concludes the series of new life with the ultimate proof of God's power to turn death into life. It would be untruthful to celebrate the joy of Easter without the sadness of Good Friday. The despair of Good Friday may at first seem an inappropriate theme to deal with at something as light-hearted as Messy Church, but the story is not whole without it: we need to know that Jesus goes through the worst times with us as well as the good times.

FOOD

Lamb burgers in pitta bread with salad

Have an echo of the traditional Passover meal. Make a tabletop display of the following items:

✛ Horseradish sauce (bitter herbs),
✛ Salt water
✛ Haroseth paste (apple sauce)
✛ Lamb bone (cooked)
✛ Matzo or unleavened bread
✛ Red wine or red fruit juice
✛ Large white candle

Have a child carry round each item as it's mentioned, so that everyone can see it and perhaps taste it. Start the meal by lighting the candle. Give out copies of these questions and answers to children and adults and use the relevant question and answer as each item is carried round.

Question 1 **Why have we got bitter herbs to eat today?**
Answer 1 The bitter herbs remind us of the bitterness of slavery. They remind us of when God's people were slaves in Egypt long, long ago.

Question 2 **Why is there salt water to taste today?**
Answer 2 The salt water reminds us of the tears God's people cried when they were slaves in Egypt.

Question 3 **Why have we got this haroseth paste today?**
Answer 3 This sauce reminds us of the mud that God's people had to use to make bricks with when they were slaves in Egypt.

Question 4 **Why have we got lamb to eat today?**

Answer 4   The lamb reminds us of the lamb's blood that
protected the houses of God's people in Egypt, so that
the angel of death passed over them and didn't hurt
them. It also reminds us that Jesus is the Lamb of God
who died for us on Good Friday so that we could be
friends with God.

Question 5 **Why have we got flat bread to eat today?**

Answer 5   The bread reminds us of the way God rescued his
people from Egypt. They had to leave in such a hurry
that there was no time for the bread to rise. It also
reminds us that Jesus took bread at his Passover meal
and broke it and gave it to his friends, saying, 'Take, eat,
this is my body, broken for you. Do this to remember
me.'

Question 6 **Why is there wine to drink today?**

Answer 6   The wine reminds us of God's blessings, when he
rescued his people from Egypt and took them to a land
full of good things. It also reminds us that Jesus took a
cup of wine and said to his friends, 'This is my blood,
poured out for you. Do this to remember me.'

Finally, the leader says, 'We eat this food tonight to remember God's
rescue of his people at Passover and at Easter time and the way he
guides us still today. Let's give thanks to God together.

All together, say, '3 2 1, 1 2 3, Thank you, God, for all our tea.'

ACTIVITIES

Egg people

You will need: Hard-boiled eggs, egg box cups (cut from cardboard egg boxes), colouring materials, scraps of felt, feathers, googly eyes, PVA glue

Hard-boil the eggs well in advance and have a range of things with which to decorate them as people, as listed above.

Talk about
Talk about the egg as a symbol of new life and of the stone that was rolled away from the tomb.

Chalice

You will need: Clean, empty yoghurt pots, cotton reels (one per two yoghurt pots), orange or gold tissue paper, PVA glue (thinned with water), paintbrushes, gold or orange poster paint, small plastic gems or sequins, string

Stick a yoghurt pot by its base on to each end of a cotton reel to make the basic shape of a goblet. Cover the entire goblet with ripped-up pieces of orange or gold tissue paper, dipped in watered-down glue. Decorate with gems or sequins and string dipped in gold or orange paint, glued round the top and bottom rims to give a chased metal effect.

Talk about
Talk about the Last Supper.

Decorated crosses

> **You will need**: Mediumweight card, art materials, PVA glue,
> scissors, pictures of different cross designs (books or the
> Internet are a good source)

You can either prepare some simple cross outlines on card for everyone to decorate or use one of the brilliant ideas from *A-cross the World*
by Martyn Payne and Betty Pedley (Barnabas, 2004).

Talk about
Talk about why the cross is the most important symbol for Christians.

Small Easter gardens

> **You will need**: Paper plates, cardboard egg boxes, garden
> items (moss, flowers, gravel and small stones), PVA glue

On a paper plate, use moss, flowers, gravel and stones to make a
miniature garden with a garden tomb.

Talk about
Talk about the events of Maundy Thursday through to Easter Day.

Large Easter garden

> **You will need**: Groundsheet or large plastic tray, turf, garden
> boulders (from a garden centre), pieces of rough wood, gravel

Make a large Easter garden for display in your church, school or
library. For the base, use anything from, for example, a plastic tray

for holding loaves from the supermarket bakery to a groundsheet. Decorate with turf or false grass, a cave made out of rocks, a hill with three crosses on it and a gravel path threading through the scenes.

Talk about

Talk about the sadness of Good Friday and the joy of Easter Day.

Edible nests

> **You will need**: Shredded Wheat breakfast cereal, cooking chocolate, bun cases, chocolate or sugar mini eggs

Mix together crumbled Shredded Wheat cereal with melted chocolate and form into a nest shape in a bun case. Put three or four little chocolate eggs in the nest.

Talk about

Talk about Easter eggs and new life.

Free range picture

> **You will need**: Lining wallpaper (unpasted), art materials

Invite everyone to draw his or her favourite part of the Easter story on to a big sheet of backing paper. It doesn't matter if you have lots of crosses or 16 Marys.

Talk about

Talk about which part of the Good Friday or Easter story is the most important part and which part people like best.

Palm crosses

You will need: Sheets of A4 paper, pencils, rulers, scissors, sticky tape

Make palm crosses out of strips of paper (see page 207 for instructions).

Talk about
Talk about Palm Sunday.

Rolling the stone

You will need: Marbles, poster paint in a variety of colours, lining wallpaper (unpasted)

Roll marbles in poster paint, then roll them over paper to leave a pattern.

Talk about
Talk about the stone being rolled away from Jesus' tomb.

Purses

You will need: Felt, embroidery silks, darning needles, iron-on Velcro or buttons, sequins, PVA glue, chocolate coins

Make a purse out of a rectangle of felt. Draw two lines across the width so that the length is divided into thirds. Fold over on one line and sew up the edges with running stitch. The remaining third forms the flap, which can be secured with some iron-on Velcro or a button and buttonhole. Decorate with sequins, glued or sewn on. Put a silver chocolate coin inside each purse.

Talk about

Talk about Jesus being betrayed for 30 pieces of silver. Talk about how much we are worth and how much he is worth.

CELEBRATION

Setting up the church or worship space

> **You will need:** A cross, a model or picture of the empty tomb, pencils, Post-it notes, an egg (for the talk), PowerPoint loaded with digital pictures of finished artwork (optional), samples of artwork from each activity station

Have a cross and a model or picture of the empty tomb at the front of the worship space. If you are using PowerPoint, have it ready to display photos of artwork as everyone arrives. Give everyone a pencil and two Post-It notes as they come in.

Song selection

Make way (*Kidsource 1*, 249)
I will offer up my life (*Songs of Fellowship 2*, 851)
I believe in Jesus (*Kidsource 1*, 122)
He is the same (Kingsway CD series songbook, 250, or Kingsway *Songs for Children*, 81)
Jesus, be the centre (*Songs of Fellowship 3*, 1377)
God is big, God is great (*Great Big God 3*, Vineyard CD)
I'm special (*Kidsource 1*, 62)

Talk

Sometimes we have to go through really bad times in life. They might be times when everything seems to go wrong. Perhaps people treat us unfairly or let us down. Perhaps something very painful happens. Perhaps our whole life seems as dead as a stone. (*Hold up an egg*)

The Easter story tells us that, although terrible things happen, they're not the end of the story. Jesus went through a terrible time in that last week. The leaders of Jerusalem ganged up against him. He was let down by his closest friends. He was punished for something he didn't do and he had to die a painful death. Then he was put in a cave with a big stone in front of it.

But... I wonder if you've spotted it? This might look like a stone, but actually it's an egg. Is an egg always dead? No—it looks dead, but one day it might break open to let a new chick be born. And although Jesus was dead and buried, on Easter Sunday he came back to life, breaking out of the grave just as the chick breaks out of the egg. So, after all the sadness and pain came a bigger joy than anyone could possibly have imagined. Jesus was alive again! Now he can be with us for ever and ever!

Prayer response

Invite everyone to use one of the two Post-It notes to write or draw something that makes them sad, that they would like tell God about. On the other, invite them to write or draw something that makes them happy, that they would like to thank God for. Stick the sad notes to the cross and stick the happy notes to the empty tomb. Bring all the prayers together with a short concluding prayer.

Final blessing

Lord, thank you that you loved us so much that you gave your life to rescue us. Help us to love each other and give each other a new start when things go wrong. Amen

Messy Grace

May the grace of our Lord Jesus Christ *(Hold out your hands as if expecting a present)*
And the love of God *(Put your hands on your heart)*
And the fellowship of the Holy Spirit *(Hold hands)*
Be with us all now and for ever. Amen! *(Raise hands together on the word 'Amen')*

UNIT 12

New life in the Spirit (Pentecost)

This unit could be a one-off, although it ties into the theme of new life. We combined our first birthday celebration (a whole year of Messy Church!) with the celebration of Pentecost, the Church's birthday.

AIM

To explore the theme of celebration and discover who the Spirit is through the symbols of wind and fire.

BIBLE BACKGROUND (Acts 2:1–13)

The story of the coming of the Holy Spirit to the first disciples was an experience that they could only describe with the images of fire and wind. There is also the occurrence of speaking in different languages and of the beginning of the early church—which is why this event has come to mark the Church's birthday.

Here we have Jesus coming in power through his Spirit as he had promised, breaking down the old barriers between humans and God that were set up in the story of the tower of Babel. He turns the cosy group of disciples into a missionary community that will change the world. He gives them confidence, courage and the power to proclaim the kingdom through word and miracles, just as Jesus himself did.

Our focus is on understanding a little of the Holy Spirit through the images of fire and wind: they help us understand the invisible power of God changing the world. There is also a strong element of celebration—expressing joy that we can receive the same Spirit all these years later, demonstrating that the Church marks the season with a festival and reinforcing the idea that when we talk about God's kingdom, it's often in terms of a party.

If you're following through the birthday theme, consider giving small gifts to everyone, including adults. For example, BRF publish small books for children. For adults, you could buy a small glass nightlight holder and scented nightlight or a small notebook or bar of soap, and have fun attaching a suitable Bible verse. A balloon, party popper (if the person is old enough) and the cake they've decorated themselves (see below) make up a good party bag.

FOOD

Pasta with Bolognese sauce, grated cheese and peas

Dish out the pasta from the kitchen on to plates and carry it to the seated people. On the tables, have separate bowls of sauce, peas and grated cheese. If you try to serve meat, peas and pasta from the kitchen, it takes hours.

ACTIVITIES

Individual birthday cakes

You will need: Ready-made fairy cakes (see recipe on page 62), butter icing (add icing sugar to softened butter or margarine until you have a soft dropping consistency), cake decorations, birthday candles and holders

Have plain fairy cakes ready to ice with butter icing and sprinkles or similar decorations. Add a birthday candle and holder to each completed cake.

Talk about

Talk about Pentecost being the day the Church celebrates its birthday, because that's when Jesus' Holy Spirit came to the first disciples.

Candle holders

> **You will need:** Oasis (florist's foam), clean plastic lids (from food containers, such as crisps and dips), tissue paper, florist's tape, thin candles, artificial flowers, florist's ribbon

Squares of oasis on plastic lids form the basis of the candle holders. Cover the lids with tissue paper if necessary. Tape the oasis square on to the lid and stick a household candle or birthday cake candle into the oasis. Decorate oasis with artificial flowers and florist's ribbon.

NB: Issue fire warnings and make sure the decorations are low and not able to catch fire, especially if using birthday cake candles.

Talk about

Talk about the way the first disciples saw something like flames above each other's heads—a sign that Jesus' Spirit was with them.

Windmills

> **You will need:** Squares of paper measuring 15cm x 15cm, a pin with a bead head, a small round bead, a thin wooden stick (dowelling or garden cane are ideal)

Make paper windmills to represent the wind of the Holy Spirit (see page 208 for diagram).

Talk about
Talk about the noise the first disciples heard when Jesus' Spirit came—like a roaring wind.

Windsocks

You will need: Sheets of cellophane or tissue paper, PVA glue, pipe cleaners, strips of tissue paper (to make streamers), string

Make a windsock by forming tissue paper or cellophane into a cone shape. Stick a pipe cleaner circle at both ends, one circle made from a whole pipe cleaner and the other from half a pipe cleaner. Glue streamers on to the narrow end and attach three pieces of string to the wide end to tie it to a tree or post.

Talk about
Talk about the way you can't see the wind, but you know it's there because of the effect it has on trees, grass, hats and... windsocks!

Wind chimes

You will need: Small lengths of bamboo cane, string, strong card (12cm in diameter, pre-cut with five slits around the outside and a hole in the middle), sticky tape

Make a wind chime by threading string through the middle of each of five differing lengths of bamboo cane and securing at the bottom end with sticky tape. Draw the tops of the strings together by fixing them evenly around a circle of strong card and taping in place. Thread a further string through the middle of the card and hang the chime where the wind will catch it.

Talk about

Talk about how the wind has power, even though you can't see it.

Blow painting

You will need: Drinking straws, lining wallpaper (unpasted), poster paint

Use straws to blow poster paint across paper in dribbly patterns.

Talk about

Talk about the way your breath is like wind, and how God's Holy Spirit is like his breath.

Calligraphy

You will need: Good-quality writing paper, calligraphy pens, calligraphy inks in a variety of colours (including black)

Encourage people to write their own name in calligraphy and to illustrate their initial with a picture or pattern that says something about them and their interests.

Talk about

Talk about the way medieval monks (who used to copy out the Bible by hand) showed how much they loved it by making it look as beautiful as they could on the page.

Kites

You will need: Lightweight card, art materials, string, strips of tissue paper

Cut out kite shapes from card, draw the crossbars, decorate with smiley faces or patterns and have real string tails on to which you tie bows of tissue paper. Use any that aren't taken home as the border for a display of the languages in the activity below.

Talk about

Talk about the excitement of a windy day and the fun of flying kites.

Decorated languages

You will need: Sheets of A4 paper, writing and colouring materials, coloured stickers, lining paper, PVA glue

Write 'Praise the Lord' in several languages in hollow chunky lettering on sheets of paper. (You'll find some in the 'Ideas' section of the Barnabas website, under Pentecost.) Other people can colour the letters in or decorate them with stickers. Then put them on display with a kite border (see activity above).

Talk about

Talk about how people of different countries can praise God in different ways. Think about your overseas missionary links. How would the people in those countries say, 'Praise the Lord'?

Paper aeroplanes

You will need: Sheets of A4 paper

Fold the paper in half lengthways. Open the paper out again and fold down the top two corners on the short end so that they meet at the centre fold. Now fold the triangle at the top of the paper down along its base, so that the point lies along the centre fold. Take the top two corners and fold them to meet at the middle fold, halfway between the top edge and the tip of the point. Fold up the point so that it covers the corners where they meet at the centre fold. Now fold the model in half with the locking triangle on the outside of the fold. Finally, with the fold at the bottom of the model, fold the 'wings' down so that their edges lie along the bottom of the plane.

Talk about
Talk about how, in Jesus' time, there weren't any aeroplanes and there wasn't much paper either!

CELEBRATION

Setting up the church or worship space

You will need: Red balloons and streamers, paper planes, pencils, PowerPoint loaded with digital pictures of finished artwork (optional), samples of artwork from each activity station

Decorate the worship space with balloons and streamers so that the party theme continues. If possible, keep all the decorations red to tie in with the fire theme. If you are using PowerPoint, have it ready to display photos of artwork as everyone comes in. Make sure everyone has a paper plane as they come in. Have spare planes ready for those who haven't got one. Give everyone a pencil.

Song selection

Walk in the light (*Kidsource 1*, 334)
We praise God (*Kidsource 1*, 360)
We are marching (*Kidsource 1*, 350)
Help me be your eyes, Lord Jesus (Doug Horley, *Humungous Song Book*, 25)

Talk

If this is the first birthday of your Messy Church group, say, 'What have we made today? Some things to do with birthdays—because it's Messy Church's first birthday. Some things we've made are to do with wind. Some are to do with flames. Some are to do with praising God in different languages.'

Explain that all these things tie in with another birthday that we're celebrating today—the birthday of the Church, which is also called Pentecost. It's the day when God gave a wonderful birthday present —the present of his Spirit.

If this is not the first birthday of your Messy Church group, just explain that the things all tie in to the Church's birthday.

On the day when the church began, all Jesus' friends were together, waiting for the present that Jesus had promised. Suddenly they heard a noise like a great whooshing wind that filled the house.

Make the sound!

Then they saw what looked like flames of fire that separated and came to rest on each of them, but didn't burn them.

Make 'flames' with your hands above the head of the person next to you.

The Spirit of God had come and was filling each one, all the women and men and children.

They all began to celebrate and praise God, but in a very surprising way. The Spirit enabled them to do something they'd never done before—to praise God in lots of different languages that they'd never learnt.

God still gives his Holy Spirit today to everyone who believes in Jesus, so we can praise God and do things for God that we'd never be able to do on our own.

Let's praise God and celebrate the birthday of the Church / Messy Church and the gift of God's Holy Spirit.

Prayer response

All write prayers on paper planes. Throw the planes into the air on the count of three. Pick up one that lands near you and, on the count of three, read out the prayers altogether.

Final blessing

Lord, thank you that through your Holy Spirit you are with your people throughout the world and throughout history. Help us to live as one family, loving each other through thick and thin. Amen

Messy Grace

May the grace of our Lord Jesus Christ *(Hold out your hands as if expecting a present)*
And the love of God *(Put your hands on your heart)*
And the fellowship of the Holy Spirit *(Hold hands)*
Be with us all now and for ever. Amen! *(Raise hands together on the word 'Amen')*

Bible landscapes

A series on biblical scenes and themes

Bible mountains

AIM

To see the significance of mountains, hills and lonely places for Jesus and others in the Bible.

BIBLE BACKGROUND

While the Protestant side of me argues that I can meet God any time, any place, any where, there is a strong case for saying that mountains play an important part in our encounters with God. For example, they could be seen as a symbolic halfway meeting point between heaven and earth, such as in the story of Moses and the Ten Commandments (Exodus 19:16—20:17) or the transfiguration (Mark 9:2–8). They also serve as places where you can escape from the rest of the world and meet God in the solitude and beauty, as Jesus did when he went off to pray in Luke 6:12, or Elijah when he hid in a cave on a mountain (1 Kings 19:1–9). I suppose, too, that mountains are significant definite landmarks and are easy to associate with stories: Elijah on Mount Carmel (1 Kings 18:20–39), Jesus' crucifixion on Golgotha (John 19:16–17) or Jerusalem being known as Mount Zion (2 Samuel 5:9). The theme of mountains is a strong link between Old and New Testament stories.

FOOD

Ham, wedges and peas

Serve wedges from the kitchen and have ham and peas on the tables.

ACTIVITIES

Mouthwatering mountains

> **You will need:** Paper plates, green glacé icing, ice cream cones, chocolate sprinkles, jelly babies

On a paper plate, pour green glacé icing over an upturned ice cream cone. Pour chocolate sprinkles on top (these are the remains of the loaves and fishes) and stick five (or fewer) jelly babies round the mountain to represent the 5000 people.

Talk about
Talk about picnics you've had on mountaintops or hillsides and link this idea to the story of Jesus feeding the five thousand in John 6:1–13.

Tablets of soap

> **You will need:** Cheap bars of soap, cocktail sticks or clay-modelling tools

Using cocktail sticks or modelling tools, carve a commandment on a bar of soap.

Talk about

Talk about how scary and awe-inspiring storms on mountains can be, and remind everyone of the awesome noise and earthquakes on the mountain where Moses met God to receive the Ten Commandments (Exodus 19:16—20:17).

Elijah's fire

> **You will need:** Sheets of sugar paper, tissue paper in red, orange, yellow and brown, grey and white colouring crayons, cotton wool balls, PVA glue, scissors

Stick tissue paper flames over strips of brown tissue paper. Draw smoke with the crayons and add clouds of cotton wool balls to make a fire collage.

Talk about

Talk about the bonfire that God gave Elijah when he prayed for a sign (1 Kings 18:36–38).

How lovely on the mountains are the footprints

> **You will need:** An old baby bath, old sponges or towels, powder paint, lining wallpaper (unpasted), flipchart, writing implements, bowls of clean, soapy water, old towels or kitchen paper

Fill an old baby bath with a layer of sponges or old towel and drench them in paint. Spread out a long piece of paper on the floor, leading up to a flipchart. People tread in the paint with bare feet, make footprints on the paper up to the flipchart and write or draw on some good news they've had recently. Have a means of washing and drying feet nearby.

Talk about

Talk about a time when you've had some good news and about the way news was carried in Bible times by runners. When there was good news in the message, the messenger was really welcome, such as in Isaiah 52:7. Talk about the good news that we can take to people when we tell them what Jesus has done for us.

Lilies of the field

> **You will need:** Coloured tissue paper, mediumweight card, green felt, scissors or pinking shears

Cut out circles of coloured tissue paper and, holding two or three together, poke your finger into the centre to make them into a flower shape. Then glue the shape on to a card and add felt stalks and leaves. Encourage everyone to make frilly edges, or zigzag or ripped ones, or whatever their originality inspires them to do.

Talk about

Talk about how Jesus doesn't want us to worry about silly things that don't really matter. In the Sermon on the Mount, he tells us not to worry about what we wear. If we look at the flowers in the fields, we can see that God gives them beautiful petals, so of course he'll give us what we need (Matthew 5:25–34).

Snakepit

> **You will need:** Wide card tubes, old washing-up gloves, scraps of paper, PVA glue, hand cream or moisturiser

Cover up one end of a cardboard tube, wide enough to fit a hand into. Cut snakes out of rubbery plastic material (such as the fingers of old washing-up gloves) and glue on a forked tongue made from paper. Smear the snakes with a few drops of hand cream or moisturiser and hide them in the tube. Challenge someone to put their hand into your 'cobra's nest' and feel what's in there.

Talk about

Talk about God's kingdom being a place where there will be no danger. That kingdom isn't here yet, but it will come. It will be like a 'holy mountain'. It will be so safe that you'll even be able to put your hand into a snake's nest (Isaiah 11:8) and the snake won't bite you.

Prayer pots

You will need: Plastic flowerpots, coloured stickers, strips of wrapping paper, lightweight card, pens or pencils

Decorate two plastic pots with stickers and wrapping paper strips or similar. Cut out six or more small pieces of card. Write one name on each piece of card and fold it in half. Then place all the cards in one of the pots. The names should be of people you'd like to pray for regularly. Use the pots during the week: pick a card out of one pot, pray for that person and then place the card in the second pot.

Talk about

Talk about finding a quiet place to enjoy being with God. Even Jesus went up a hill on his own to pray (Luke 6:12).

God's holy mountain collage

You will need: An old single bed sheet or piece of hessian fabric, a piece of fabric in dark purple or green, Blu-tack or drawing pins, a selection of nature magazines, scraps of paper, poster paint, brushes, PVA glue

Add a vertical triangular dark purple or green shape to the sheet or hessian to make a wallhanging that echoes the mountain theme. Stencil on, or cut out of magazines, all sorts of happy animals and people to live on the mountain.

Talk about

Talk about what it's like living with animals. In God's kingdom, people and animals will live happily together as they did in the story of creation.

Olives

You will need: Small pieces of bread, olive oil in a shallow dish, stoned olives, cocktail sticks, items made of olive wood

Have some small pieces of bread to dip into olive oil to try, and some different varieties of olives on cocktail sticks to sample. If you have anything made of olive wood, bring that for everyone to hold and look at. Obviously, watch out for food allergies.

Talk about

Talk about the Mount of Olives in Jerusalem. King David wept there when he had been betrayed, and put himself in God's hands (2 Samuel 15:30). Many years later, Jesus prayed there and also put himself in God's hands after Judas had betrayed him (Luke 22:39–42).

Mount Zion

You will need: Sheets of sugar paper, poster paints, brushes, jars of clean water

Read Psalm 48:1–3. What picture do these words give you in your imagination? Can you paint what you imagine?

Talk about

Talk about mountains you have climbed, especially beautiful ones. Say that Jerusalem was built on Mount Zion and, when Jewish people came to Jerusalem, they would look forward to seeing the mountain in the middle of the city. David wrote songs about it.

CELEBRATION

Setting up the church or worship space

You will need: PowerPoint loaded with digital pictures of finished artwork (optional), samples of artwork from each activity station

Have some mountaineering ropes and equipment on display around the worship space, as well as posters of mountains from different parts of the world. If you are using PowerPoint, have it ready to display photos of artwork as everyone comes in.

Song selection

Prayer is like a telephone (*Kidsource 1*, 286)
Wonderful Lord (Doug Horley, *Humungous Song Book*, 98)
King of love (Doug Horley, *Humungous Song Book*, 50)

Jesus, Jesus (*Kidsource 1*, 204)
Faith as small as a mustard seed (Doug Horley *Humungous Song Book*, 15)
Over the mountains (*Songs of Fellowship* 2, 975)

Talk

Ask: Who's climbed a mountain?

Jesus used to like going up mountains to pray to his Father (Matthew 14:23). One day, Jesus took Peter, James and John up a mountain to pray (Luke 9:28). While they were there, they saw Jesus' face shining and his clothes bright as a flash of lightning, and they knew he was God's special son. On another mountainside, Jesus taught his followers how to live in God's kingdom (Matthew 5:1).

Mountains are… high! You get amazing views from the top. And they're… dangerous! Lots of people have accidents on mountains. Mountains are… awesome! We gasp at their majesty and beauty. They are… huge! They remind us how small we are and how great the God is who made them.

Refer to local mountains or the lack of them and ask where you might go to find a mountain to climb. For example: 'There are no mountains near here, but we do have hills like Butser Hill. It's really good to climb a hill and spend a moment thanking God for everything you see from the top of it.'

Next time you climb a hill, stop, be still and say a prayer as Jesus did, thanking God for the wonderful things he's made and the even greater wonder that his Son, Jesus, died on a cross at the top of a hill to show us and teach how much God loves us.

Prayer response

Make a mountain shape with your arms. As we think about going UP the mountain, let's call out things to thank and praise God for…

As we think about coming DOWN, let's call out the names of people we want God to bless and help…

Final blessing

Lord, thank you for mountains that have brought people close to you throughout the world and throughout history. Help us to set time aside to be with you in the quietness of our hearts and the beauty of your creation. Amen

Messy Grace

May the grace of our Lord Jesus Christ *(Hold out your hands as if expecting a present)*
And the love of God *(Put your hands on your heart)*
And the fellowship of the Holy Spirit *(Hold hands)*
Be with us all now and for ever. Amen! *(Raise hands together on the word 'Amen')*

UNIT 14

Bible roads

AIM

To explore the symbolism of roads.

BIBLE BACKGROUND

'Roads' is another strong theme in the Bible. God's people are often depicted as being on a journey, both physically and spiritually—from Adam and Eve's journey out of Eden (Genesis 3:23) to Paul's final missionary journeys (Acts 28:16–31). It is an important image for us to understand today. A journey gives us a starting and a finishing point—a destination. We are not aimless and passive in life; we have a purpose and a goal and a way of getting there.

FOOD

Baguette pizza and salad

Serve pizza from the kitchen and have salad and garlic bread on the tables.

ACTIVITIES

Road pictures

You will need: Pavement chalks in a variety of colours

Some people say that life is like a journey. Find an area outside where everyone has space to chalk on the ground. (We used the grids of the car park.) In groups, chalk a picture of your road story using pavement chalks.

Talk about

Talk about different Bible stories with journeys in them. If you need some starters, suggest some of the following: Adam and Eve walking out of Eden (Genesis 3:23); Abraham and Sarah (Genesis 12:1–5); Joseph (Genesis 37:12–28); Moses leading the Israelites out of Egypt and through the desert (Exodus 13:17–22); Ruth and Naomi journeying to Bethlehem (Ruth 1:1–19); the people of God travelling into exile in Babylon (2 Kings 25:1–12); Mary and Joseph travelling to Bethlehem (Luke 2:1–7); the good Samaritan (Luke 10:30–35); the journey to and from home of the prodigal son (Luke 15:11–32); the road to Emmaus (Luke 24:13–35); Paul's missionary journeys recorded in Acts... to name but a few.

Treasure hunt

You will need: A piece of paper with a list of things to find (see below) for each person

Send everyone round a safe area with a list of things to find, such as an oak leaf, feather, twig, flower, something yellow, pebble and so on.

Talk about

Talk about journeys that have a particular goal.

Lollipop ladies

> **You will need:** Lollipops, large round sweets or biscuits, sweetie eyes and lips, glacé icing

Stick sweetie eyes and sweet lips on to a lollipop, large round sweet or biscuit, using runny icing.

Talk about

Talk about the danger of crossing the road and how to cross safely.

Road signs

> **You will need:** Pre-cut card triangles, red card or paper strips, PVA glue, black paper, black felt-tipped pens, lolly sticks (from craft shops), string (optional)

Glue red borders made from card or paper strips on to the card triangles. Design your own road signs on the triangles, using black paper cut-outs or black felt-tipped pens. Tape the sign on to a stick or make a hole in the top and thread string through so that it can be hung on a door handle or pin. What might it mean on your Christian journey? For example, 'No U-turns' = never turn back! 'Bumpy road' = a difficult time lies ahead of you, and so on.

Talk about

Talk about the Christian life being like a journey: we're always moving on to the next adventure. Talk about symbols: the way a picture can represent an idea or command.

Car design

> **You will need:** Empty cardboard boxes, junk art materials, PVA glue, ribbon or similar

Make stand-in cars out of cardboard boxes, with junk accessories glued on. Fasten over the shoulders with straps of ribbon or similar. Hold a Formula 1 race.

Talk about
Talk about how people travel around in cars today, while in biblical times they would have had to walk or ride an animal. Journeys would have been much slower.

Life journey maps

> **You will need:** Large sheets of paper, drawing equipment

Draw an illustrated map of your life as if it were a road with the landmarks marked on it clearly.

Talk about
Talk about how we are on a journey from birth onwards.

People on the road

> **You will need:** Lining wallpaper (unpasted), drawing equipment

Draw a large road down the middle of a long piece of paper. Draw and label people from the Bible stories on their journey down the road as if they're all going the same way at the same time. Draw on speech bubbles to show what they're saying to each other.

Talk about
Talk about all the people on the move throughout the Bible.

Good Samaritan

You will need: White toilet rolls

Wrap up a friend, child or parent in toilet paper bandages.

Talk about
Retell the story of the good Samaritan (Luke 10:25–37).

Road to Emmaus

You will need: Shoe box lids, mediumweight card, drawing materials, PVA glue

Make a road scene on a box lid and make paper figures out of folded card to be the two disciples and Jesus. Draw Jerusalem with an empty cross at one end and the house at Emmaus at the other. Use the scene to act out the story.

Talk about
Retell the story of Jesus appearing to the two disciples on the road to Emmaus (Luke 24:13–35).

Sandals

You will need: Felt or strong fabric, marker pens, string or ribbon, scissors

Make some sandals out of felt or strong fabric. Draw round the sole of your foot, leaving a wide border. Cut out the shape and tie it on to your foot with a long piece of string or ribbon. You could make holes round the edge and lace it on or just wrap the ribbon round and round your foot and the sandal.

Talk about
Talk about the way people in biblical times would have either worn sandals or gone barefoot for their journeys.

CELEBRATION

Setting up the church or worship space

You will need: Cones or road signs (see below), PowerPoint loaded with digital pictures of finished artwork (optional), samples of artwork from each activity station

Borrow some cones and road signs from the highways department of your local council or from the police to decorate the worship space. If you are using PowerPoint, have it ready to display photos of artwork as everyone comes in.

Song selection

Jesus, be the centre (*Songs of Fellowship 3*, 1377)
I will offer up my life (*Songs of Fellowship 2*, 851)

Lord, I lift your name on high (Doug Horley, *Humungous Song Book*, 59)

I'm gonna click, click, click (*Kidsource 1*, 150)

Talk

Use pictures or PowerPoint for this talk.

Life is like a journey on a long road. Sometimes the journey is difficult or dangerous, just as roads can be difficult to cross. Road signs can help us find the way safely.

Show a lollipop sign.

Who would you see carrying this sign?

A lollipop lady or man (school crossing patrol) carries this sign to show us the safe place to cross the road. He or she stands in the middle of the road, holds out his or her arms and stops the traffic, so it's safe for us to cross.

Now hold out your arms like a lollipop person. That reminds me of another sign—a sign that we see in church, that some of us wear. Yes, it's the sign of the cross. Jesus stretched out his arms wide on the cross so that we can be safe on our journey through life. He loves to stop us doing things that will hurt ourselves or other people and he loves to stop other people hurting us, too. Jesus promises to be our guide and to show us the right way, if we follow him.

Prayer response

Stretch out your arms again like a lollipop person. Now think of someone who needs God's help.

Leader: As we think of these people we know, Jesus, please stretch out your arms of love to help them.

All: Amen

Final blessing

Lord, thank you that you have guided your people throughout the world and throughout history. Help us to follow you on our journey through life. Amen

Messy Grace

May the grace of our Lord Jesus Christ *(Hold out your hands as if expecting a present)*
And the love of God *(Put your hands on your heart)*
And the fellowship of the Holy Spirit *(Hold hands)*
Be with us all now and for ever. Amen! *(Raise hands together on the word 'Amen')*

UNIT 15

Bible seasides

This unit is one of a series on biblical scenes and themes. The session links in well with summer holidays on the beach.

AIM

To explore the themes of seaside stories in the Bible.

BIBLE BACKGROUND

In the Bible, the uncontrollable nature of the sea is traditionally associated with the powers of chaos and evil and the symbolism of moving through chaos into order. This is evident right from the very beginning of time, when God created everything out of the chaos of an earth that was 'barren, with no form of life... under a roaring ocean covered with darkness' (Genesis 1:1–2). Again, in Exodus we find order rising out of chaos as Moses leads the Israelites out of Egypt, through the Reed Sea and into the promised land (Exodus 13:17—14:30).

The symbolism of the exodus story has strong links with the symbolism of baptism in the New Testament, from Jesus' baptism (Matthew 3:13–17) to our own (Romans 6:3–4). Throughout the Gospels, Jesus is in authority over the chaos of water—turning water into wine (John 2:1–11), controlling the wind and the waves (Luke 8:22–25) and using the symbolism of fishing (Luke 5:1–11), building on sand (Matthew 7:24–27) and drawing water from a well (John 4:3–26) to explore the very nature of God.

FOOD

Fish fingers, new potatoes and peas

Serve the fish fingers from the kitchen and put the vegetables in dishes on tables.

ACTIVITIES

Seaside cards

You will need: Blue card, scissors, colouring and drawing materials, PVA glue

Make a seaside card using pieces of blue card cut into wavy shapes, boat shapes and seagull shapes. Encourage everyone to send his or her card to someone to wish them a happy and restful holiday. If you were feeling cheeky you could write a misquote of Isaiah 40:30–31:

'Those who trust the Lord will find new strength.
They will be strong like seagulls (eagles) soaring upwards on wings...'
Happy Holiday!

Talk about
Talk about the fun and peace of being by the sea.

Decorated frames

You will need: Cheap wooden picture frames, sea shells, PVA glue, sheets of paper printed with Genesis 2:3 (see below), colouring and drawing materials

Decorate a wooden frame with shells. Have computer printouts of the (NIV) Bible verse: 'God blessed the seventh day and made it holy, because on it he rested.' Above the verse, leave a space for people to draw themselves on holiday or to stick a holiday snap.

Talk about
Talk about how the word 'holidays' comes from 'holy days'—God likes us to rest and be well and take time to enjoy the world and each other.

Lim-pets

You will need: Limpet shells, mediumweight card or foam shapes, PVA glue

Make pets out of large limpet shells, with eyes, ears and feet made of card or foam shapes and glued on. Encourage people to name their lim-pet.

Talk about
Talk about the wonderful creatures and shells we find by the seaside, and how God has made them all different.

Fish mosaics

You will need: Plastic party plates, tissue paper, PVA glue (diluted with water), brushes, card in a variety of colours, scissors

Take a sturdy plastic plate and coat it with tissue paper, pasted on with diluted PVA glue, to give an interesting textured background.

Using pieces of cut-up card, glue the pieces on to the plate as a mosaic in the shape of a fish.

Talk about

Talk about Jesus giving his disciples breakfast on the beach after the resurrection (John 21:4–14).

Sand drizzling

You will need: Sheets of sugar paper, silver sand or 'sand' made using salt and poster paint (see below), PVA glue

Dribble glue on to a piece of paper in a twirly pattern. Pour sand over it and shake off the excess. You can make 'sand' with salt and poster paint. For sand colour, add a teaspoon of yellow and half a teaspoon of red paint to a 1 kg bag of salt.

Talk about

Talk about how lovely sand is to build a sandcastle with—but what would happen if you tried to build a real house on the sand?

Jonah's big fish

You will need: Mediumweight card, small boxes (for example, empty teabag boxes), drinking straws or sticks, PVA glue, sticky tape, scissors, colouring materials

Cut out two fish shapes and glue them on to either side of a small box. Make a small Jonah figure out of card and tape it on to a straw or stick. Insert the free end of the stick into the box between the two fish shapes so that you can pull Jonah in (being swallowed by the fish) and push him out (being vomited up by the fish).

Talk about
Talk about the story of Jonah and how there was nowhere he could run to get away from God.

Fishing

You will need: Pre-cut cardboard fish, paper clips, marker pen to write the words from Luke 5:10 (NRSV) on the fish, small garden canes, string, small magnets, large bowl, fizzy fish sweets

Make cardboard fish with paper clips on their mouths. Write a word from the verse 'From now on you will be catching people' on each fish and put them in a bowl. Make fishing rods from sticks with string attached and with a small magnet at the end. As people manage to catch up the fish and work out the verse, give them a small prize—a fizzy fish sweet or similar.

Talk about
Talk about how some of Jesus' followers were fishermen.

House on the rock

You will need: Pebble-sized stones, pre-cut card cube nets made from mediumweight card, felt-tipped pens, PVA glue, strips of paper with Bible verse on them (see below)

Draw windows and a door on a card net with felt-tips. Make up the net into a cube and glue the cube to a stone. On a strip of paper, write or print, 'The house on the rock stands firm (Matthew 7:25)'. Glue this strip round the stone's base.

Talk about

Talk about the story of the two builders (Matthew 7:24–27).

Fishers of people wall display

> **You will need**: Mediumweight card, pre-cut fish shapes made from heavyweight card, colouring materials, black marker pens, scissors, lining wallpaper (unpasted), PVA glue

Make some fish shapes out of card to use as templates. Ask each person to cut out a fish and decorate it with their own name. Use all the finished fish in a wall display of fish being caught in a net.

Talk about

Talk about inviting a friend along to next month's Messy Church and how that would make you like a fisherman, catching people instead of fish (Matthew 4:19). The 'fish' can then have a happy time doing art and craft, rather than just being in the sea!

Wet play

> **You will need**: Old baby bath, sheets of A4 paper, play buckets and bottles, towels

Make paper boats and sail them on the baby bath sea. (Sarah claims she's used her baby bath more since starting Messy Church than she ever did to bath babies in.) Have some play buckets and bottles to play with and towels for the inevitable consequences.

Talk about

Talk about the time Jesus calmed the storm (Luke 8:22–25).

CELEBRATION

Setting up the church or worship space

> **You will need:** Seaside items (see below), pre-cut brick shapes (see 'Prayer response'), backing paper, glue sticks, pictures of beaches and sandcastles, PowerPoint loaded with digital pictures of finished artwork (optional), samples of artwork from each activity station

Have some buckets and spades, sunshades and seaside paraphernalia to look at around the worship space. Wear a sunhat and shades and Hawaiian shirt. If you are using PowerPoint, have it ready to display photos of artwork as everyone comes in.

Song selection

Life is like a big wide ocean (*Kidsource 1*, 232)
The wise man built his house upon the rock (*Kidsource 1*, 336)
Over the mountains and the sea (*Kidsource 1*, 279)

Talk

Ask what everyone likes about the seaside. Tell a funny story about your experience by the sea when you were a child (everyone has one!) Say that you're sure everyone's spotted the theme for today: seasides. Lots of exciting things happen by the seaside in the Bible: Jonah gets thrown up out of a big fish on to a beach; Jesus calls his disciples to follow him and he tells a fantastic parable—a story with a secret— about some men on a beach.

Show pictures of beaches and sandcastles. Talk about how it's fun to play on a beach and build sandcastles, but what happens to them? They wash away when the tide comes in. So would the beach be a good place to build a house? Of course not!

Tell the story of the two builders (Matthew 7:24–27), acting it out with as much slapstick as you can comfortably insert.

Jesus told a story about someone who liked the beach so much that he decided to build a house there. It was very easy: flat, with plenty of space (*tread on a crab, choke on the smell of some smelly seaweed—pooh!*) There were good views, lots of sea air, handy for swimming and fishing (*get nipped by the crab again*). So he built his house on the beach (*hammer your thumb, cut off your foot with a saw*). Soon he had finished and he sat in his house looking out, enjoying the sun and sea air (*choke on the seaweed smell again*).

Through the window he saw someone else working, building on a rocky hill.

For the second man, it was very hard work: there was less space and the ground was hard (*drill foundations sweatily, push the wheelbarrow up the hill and let it pull you down the other side, build a brick wall with lots of sloppy cement*). It took a lot longer, but he eventually finished too, and sat looking out at the man in the house on the beach.

Both men saw dark clouds gathering. They heard the wind getting stronger (*let the children make sound effects*), they saw the tide coming in and the waves getting huge. Then the great storm broke. The wind and rain battered the house on the rock, but it stood firm.

But what was happening to the house on the beach? The wind and the waves were bashing the house on every side. It fell to bits and fell flat. The poor builder had to paddle to safety. He had lost everything.

Jesus called the person who built his house on the beach 'foolish'. Why? He called the person who built his house on the rock 'wise'. Why? Jesus said, 'Anyone who hears and obeys these words of mine is like a wise person who built a house on solid rock.' It may seem harder, but you're building your life on a firm foundation. Jesus also said, 'If you hear what I say and don't obey, you're like the foolish builder.' It may seem easier, but what you build won't withstand the storms of life.

This summer, when we go to the beach and enjoy building

sandcastles and see the waves come in and wash them away, let's remind each other of Jesus' story of the wise and foolish builders—that we need to be wise and do what Jesus says, to love him and love each other as he loves us.

Prayer response

Have some brick-sized, coloured rectangles of card or paper. Ask everybody to think of something they can do this month to obey Jesus' teaching in your area. Make a few suggestions, such as doing something to help someone else, saying something kind to somebody, spending a little time praying every day, inviting somebody else along to Messy Church and so on. They should draw or write what they plan to do on a 'brick' and then bring it up to the front as an offering. Have a large sheet of backing paper on which to glue the bricks in a wall pattern. It's good to have some quiet music playing while everyone is doing this.

Draw all the prayers together with the Lord's Prayer. (Put the words up on an OHP.)

Final blessing

Lord, thank you for the fun of holidays. Help us to enjoy your creation and love each other in the way that you have taught us to do. Amen

Messy Grace

May the grace of our Lord Jesus Christ *(Hold out your hands as if expecting a present)*
And the love of God *(Put your hands on your heart)*
And the fellowship of the Holy Spirit *(Hold hands)*
Be with us all now and for ever. Amen! *(Raise hands together on the word 'Amen')*

Instructions for making a paper boat

1. Take a sheet of A4 paper and fold it in half widthways (Figure 1).
2. Find the centre point along the folded edge of the paper and fold the corners down to meet in the middle, forming a triangle (Figure 2).
3. Open out the remaining edge of the paper and fold each side back towards the triangle, forming a hat shape (Figure 3).
4. Holding the lower edge (the 'brim' of the hat) at the centre point on both sides, open the shape out and refold it to make a diamond. Tuck the loose ends neatly under each other on both sides (Figure 4).
5. Lay the diamond shape flat and fold back the open end to match the triangle shape at the top of the diamond (Figure 5).
6. Turn the paper over and repeat with the other side (Figure 6).
7. Once again, holding the lower edge at the centre point, open the shape out and refold it to make a diamond shape (Figure 7).
8. Take hold of the outer points on both sides of the top of the diamond and gently pull them apart in an outward direction (Figure 8). This will form the boat shape, with the small centre triangle acting as a sail.
9. Gently shape the paper around the base of the sail so that the bottom of the hull is slightly flattened, allowing the boat to stand (Figure 9). The finished boat will be strong enough to float on water for a short length of time.

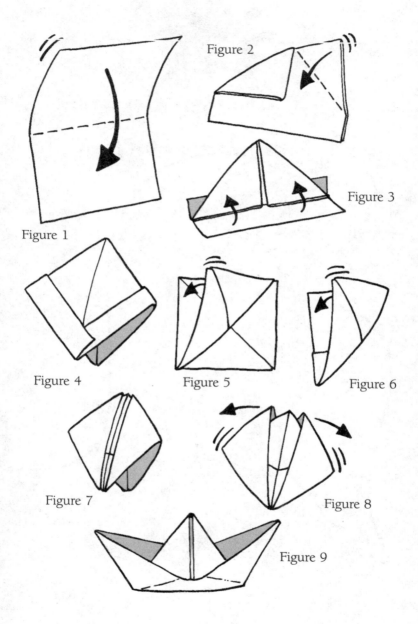

Figure 1

Figure 2

Figure 3

Figure 4

Figure 5

Figure 6

Figure 7

Figure 8

Figure 9

205

Dove